SEA ANGLING AROUND BRITAIN

The Angler's Library

SEA ANGLING
AROUND BRITAIN

by

TREVOR HOUSBY

BARRIE & JENKINS
COMMUNICA - EUROPA

First published in 1977 by
Barrie & Jenkins Ltd
24 Highbury Crescent, London N5 1RX

ISBN 0 214 20259 3

Printed in Great Britain by The Anchor Press Ltd
and bound by Wm Brendon & Son Ltd
both of Tiptree, Essex

Contents

Introduction

As an angling journalist with a series of regular columns I receive a vast amount of mail from anglers who want information on fishing venues which are out of their normal locality. This book is intended as a comprehensive answer to the sort of questions I get asked. It is a basic guide to sea angling right round Britain, dealing with coasts region by region; inshore fishing from beach, boat, pier or charter.

My work as angling consultant to several Tourist Boards has given me a unique opportunity of studying the fishing potential of many areas which have never been properly surveyed before, and I can therefore give details of both shore and boat fishing possibilities which will be of the utmost value to the anglers visiting these localities for the first time. The aim it to bypass many of the difficulties the 'honorary' angler may meet with by providing a basic knowledge of species and methods valuable in the particular area he has chosen to visit. Where possible I have recounted personal experiences which it is hoped the reader will find stimulating as well as informative.

Finally, I should like to re-emphasise points made in my previous volume in the Anglers Library – *Boat Fishing*. Take and use light tackle whenever possible, in the interests of sporting tackle; but do not neglect modern developments such as steel lines for use where tides are fierce. Above all look to your safety, and that of others. A large part of this book is addressed to those who will be trailing their own boat for launching in new waters. *Boat Fishing* will give them additional sound advice.

The South East Coast

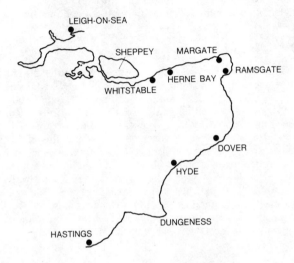

Isle of Sheppey to Hastings

Within easy travelling distance of London and many smaller towns, this section of the south coast is naturally very heavily fished. Despite this, the whole area is more than capable of yielding first-class catches, particularly during the winter months when cod and whiting shoals come right inshore to keep beach and boat anglers' rod tops knocking.

9

Sheppey

During the summer months this area is often inundated with silver eels which make a nuisance of themselves by snatching at any baited hook that comes their way. During the winter these eels disappear almost completely and boat anglers in particular often get amongst the cod in a big way.

Whitstable

Once famous for its excellent oysters, Whitstable also provides shore and boat fishermen with good mixed fishing. Shore anglers take cod, pouting, whiting, sole, dab, flounder and silver eels in good quantities during the various seasons. The shingle beach by the SWALECLIFFE sewer to the east of Tankerton is a favourite venue. In the winter this beach is particularly good for cod fishing. Other notable beaches are WHITSTABLE STREET shingle beach and LONG BEACH which is situated on the east side of the harbour. The harbour wall at Whitstable, although not always particularly rewarding, can produce the odd good catch and for this reason is well worth a visit. Boats are not easy to charter at Whitstable, although anglers can launch their own boats at HORSBRIDGE.

Herne Bay

Like Whitstable, the Herne Bay area can fish extremely well at times. To a certain extent beach anglers are limited to RECULVER BEACH and SWALECLIFFE BEACH, both of which are occasionally closed to the public. Cod, whiting, flatfish, silver eels, bass and pouting are the most common shore-caught species in this locality, although garfish and the occasional big tope can also be caught. Offshore species include skate, conger, cod, tope, whiting and dogfish. A number of charter boats operate in the Herne Bay area, although many anglers bring their own boats.

Margate

Although holiday crowds make Margate something of an angler's nightmare, night fishing or winter fishing can produce excellent catches either from the numerous beach marks or from the stone pier. The wooden pier is limited to day-time fishing only and anglers are only allowed on the lower deck. Despite the drawbacks to Margate as a shore-fishing centre, a wide and varied selection of fish can be taken, including cod, tope, bass, whiting and flatfish. Boat anglers able to get offshore away from the crowded beaches often bring in fair catches of thornback skate, tope, cod, whiting and the usual flatfish.

Ramsgate

I always think of Ramsgate as the start of the Channel cod grounds. I can remember many trips down from London in bitterly cold winter weather when boat marks situated only a few hundred yards offshore have produced a seemingly endless stream cod and codling. Ramsgate cod never grow to a vast size but what they lose in quality they certainly make up for in quantity. Lugworm always seem the best bait in this area and a bunch of big black lugworm fished on leger or paternoster usually produced a flurry of good bites, seconds after getting down to fish level. On days when bad weather made boat fishing impossible, I used to fish from the shore at PEGWELL BAY, again often with good results. Ramsgate, like Margate, is basically a holiday resort, which means that during the summer months the beaches are jam-packed with swimmers and sun-worshippers. Under conditions like this, fishing is out of the question but at night or during the winter months PEGWELL BAY, the WESTERN UNDERCLIFFE, or the MARINA SLOPES can fish well. The East and West piers are worth fishing, the West Pier in particular fishes well after dark for fair-sized conger eels. DEAL has steep-to beaches and is very much fished by the professional boatman, and is not therefore very suitable for the angler wishing to launch himself.

Dover

From the sea angler's point of view, Dover is one of the top fishing venues on the south coast. Big fish and big catches are common here, particularly during the winter-time when

11

vast packs of big cod move inshore on all fronts. Basically, Dover is a cod fishing hot-spot, for despite the fact that many other species can be caught, most anglers arrive with cod fishing in mind. There is plenty of fair fishing on local beaches and from Castle Jetty, but most shore casters go out by boat to fish the SOUTHERN BREAKWATER. Boats operate from the Admiralty Pier and from the Prince of Wales Pier to take parties of anglers out to this noted fishing spot.

The Southern Breakwater, officially a shore station, provides a sort of mixture between beach-casting and boat fishing, for although anglers still use conventional beach-casting outfits, they cast their baits out into comparatively deep water where big cod abound. I have fished the breakwater on many occasions, usually in bitterly cold weather when rough seas have made life far from comfortable. Despite inclement weather, I have usually gone back home with something to show for my efforts; although there have been many occasions when my catches have been limited to whiting, I have nearly always seen a big cod or two caught, and on many occasions, when my luck has been in, I have returned via the ferry boat with several good big cod to my credit.

I have always found the Southern Breakwater an exciting place to fish. I never know what to expect and a slight touch of a bite that appears to come from a tiny whiting can sometimes result in a really hefty cod being hooked. My best day on the breakwater produced four cod and a batch of nice whiting. It was a Saturday in December, the weather was cold, clear and still. I had journeyed down from London with the intention of putting in as many rod hours as possible. I had plenty of bait and a good supply of end tackle, for I had lost a lot of gear on past occasions and did not want to have to cut short a long session through lack of equipment.

When I arrived on the breakwater I could see from the number of displayed fish and bulging bags that a good run of fish was under way, so I did not waste any time while fixing up my tackle. In my haste I could not have tied my knots properly, for within the first ten minutes of casting out I hit a rod-bender of a bite, brought a biggish cod to the surface, only to lose it as my line came away at a trace swivel. Making my tackle up again, I checked and re-checked all knots, baited up the two hooks with big bunches of juicy lugworms and cast the whole lot out again to approximately the same place where the first fish had taken the hook. This time I had to wait for over an hour before a slight tap on the rod tip warned me that a fish of some sort was pulling at the bait. Big cod often bite very gently, in fact hungry whiting usually give a more determined bite than cod, and this gentle pull at the rod top made me think that perhaps a cod was responsible.

Picking up the rod I waited for the bite to develop. For a minute or two nothing, then another gentle tweak at the rod tip warned me that the fish was still interested in the bait. Then slowly the rod tip keeled over as the fish sucked in the bunch of worms and moved off with the bait in its jaws. Striking was a formality and as soon as I hit the fish I realised it was a good one. Big cod are poor fighters, but being heavy they pull hard, shaking their great heads from side to side in an attempt to get rid of the hook. Taking things easy, I gradually worked the fish up from the sea bed and began to coax it inshore. As usual, other anglers gathered to watch the struggle and one of these men volunteered to use the drop net that is so essential off the high breakwater.

Finally it was over, the fish lay in the bottom of the big circular net while willing hands hoisted it up to the top of the wall. That fish weighed just 18 lb, a grand catch by most shore-casting standards and more than enough to make my day. Ten minutes later I got a 10-pounder, then a succession of good, big Channel whiting. Finally in the last hour of fishing left to me I hooked and landed cod of 14 lb and 16 lb. A magnificent day's sport even by boat-fishing standards and a typical example of the kind of sport that the Southern Breakwater can produce. Many anglers have had much bigger catches than this and no doubt in future seasons the breakwater will go on producing good fish in respectable numbers. I hope so, for it is at present one of the best fishing stations anywhere along the south coast.

The ADMIRALTY PIER at Dover is famous for its big bass. Local anglers have devised and developed a unique after-dark technique for taking big bass in quantity. This method is extremely interesting, for it could work just as well round other piers and harbours, although as yet I have never heard of anyone using it elsewhere. Basically the method is simple. Using just a rod, reel, line and hook, the success of the method rests on keeping the bait floating on the surface. Somehow or other Dover bass specialists discovered that the very big bass that hang about the pier structures will eat dead fish they find floating on the surface. These Dover bass actually rise like trout to a fly and in all probability someone saw them do this, tried floating a dead fish out to them and ended up by catching big bass and developing a new technique. Most of the big bass caught on floating baits are taken at night and invariably the bait is a small, freshly-caught pouting. Pouting tend to fill up with air when being brought to the surface, consequently when used as bait they have a sort of built-in buoyancy tank which keeps them floating for long periods. Small pouting are commonly caught off the pier at Dover and anglers have formed the habit of unhooking the little fish and throwing them straight back into the water, where they float away on the tide. Local bass have obviously learned to cash in on this plentiful and easily obtainable food supply and so accept a floating dead-bait as a natural part of their normal diet.

There can be little doubt that the Admiralty Pier bass are used to feeding in this way, for when they do rise and take a floating bait, they take it with a great show of confidence which makes them very easy to hook. I am inclined to think that this technique could be adapted for use round many piers or harbour walls and for this reason anglers are advised to try the method in their own locality.

Hythe

To a certain extent Hythe is overshadowed by Dover and Dungeness. This is a pity, for beaches adjacent to Hythe can fish very well indeed. Favourite local areas range from the ROYAL MILITARY CANAL outfall along the PRINCES PARADE to the IMPERIAL HOTEL on Hythe beach. There are also miles of good fishing on the COAST ROAD (A259) which runs along close by the promenade. It is difficult to hire boats at Hythe but anglers who tow their own boats can launch them from STADE COURT in Stade Street, approximately half a mile east of the Imperial Hotel. The beaches in this area fish well for cod and whiting in the winter and skate, flatfish and small bass in the summer-time. Night fishing is best.

Dungeness

Dungeness Beach is famous both for its catches and the long-casting techniques which were devised and developed specifically for fishing it. During the summer months, Dungeness fishes well for flatfish, bass, pouting and the occasional skate. The warm-water outlet from the power station is a favourite haunt of bass and local anglers long cast dead-bait out to this boil of water in an attempt to catch these fine fish. When the bass packs are on the feed this technique can be extremely deadly and catches of forty or more bass in a single session have been recorded.

Basically, however, Dungeness is a winter cod-fishing resort and on an average weekend in November or December 500 or more anglers may night fish the beach in the hope of contacting the roving cod shoals as they move inshore in search of food. On a good night, when the cod bite readily, sport comes thick and fast. Big cod, small cod, whiting and pouting all come splashing and struggling through the surf as anglers cast, strike and wind in as fast as they can crank

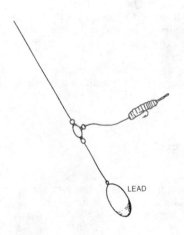

LEAD

Fig. 1 Lugworm on paternoster tackle.

a reel handle. This is exciting fishing, as anyone who has fished Dungeness beach on a good night can tell you. Lug-worm on paternoster tackle (see fig. 1) is the standard Dungeness rig and highly effective it is too.

Like most areas, Dungeness has suffered a drop in catches over the past few years, but it can fish well on occasions and most anglers that fish it regularly still report good overall catches. Dungeness is the kind of beach that springs surprises on its anglers. More than one 30-lb cod has been caught there. An off-duty policeman, who decided to bait up with a small livebait instead of the customary lugworm, promptly found himself firmly attached to a big, aggressive fish which finally turned out to be a 17-lb pollack. How or why a pollack of this size had found its way up to Dungeness, no one can say but it provided a startled policeman with a thrills-and-spills fight that he will never forget.

Boat fishing at Dungeness can be very good indeed, but, like most steep-to-shingle beaches, can be a dangerous place to launch or beach a boat. Once afloat, fishing can be first class. Dungeness produced the 84-lb conger-eel record which stood for so many years. The same angler also caught the thresher-shark record from this area, proof that the offshore grounds at Dungeness are more than capable of holding some monster fish. The boat fishing from the SOUTH FORE-LAND at Dover down to Dungeness Point is extremely good, particularly during the winter months when shoals of big cod and fine fat whiting come inshore to feed. This whole area is dangerous for small-boat work, so anyone trailing a boat down to launch it here should seek advice from a local, experienced person before making any attempt to go afloat. Accidents can happen to the best of boatmen and on a steep-to-shingle beach the slightest mistake could cause a fatality.

Hastings and St Leonards

Both resorts are popular with the holiday crowds, and so daytime beach fishing during the summer months is almost out of the question. At night, however, it is possible to get some good fishing in the area for bass, dab, whiting and, in the winter-time, cod.

Shore-fishing sites to head for are ST LEONARDS and the GULLY BEACHES, FAIRLIGHT COVE, HOOK'S HARD and GOAT

ROCKS. Bass fishing can be particularly good at Fairlight, provided you take the trouble to obtain a supply of soft-backed or peeler crab for bait. Fairlight bass tend to be totally preoccupied with eating crab and most other baits fail to interest them.

Essentially a light-tackle venue, Fairlight Cove can fish well provided you are prepared to fish hard for long hours and not worry about losing terminal tackle. The bass in this area average 4 lb to 7 lb. At times the town pier and the harbour wall can fish well but mostly the fishing here is rather patchy. Small boats can be launched at Hastings, but again conditions have to be near perfect. Boat-fishing trips can be arranged through tackle shops in the town. Skate, conger, tope, cod, whiting, dogfish and mackerel are the most common species caught.

CHAPTER 2

The South Coast

Eastbourne to Portsmouth

Eastbourne, like Hastings, can produce good results at times. Bass are again the most sought-after species and most anglers that fish this area head for BEACHY HEAD shore or BIRLING GAP.

Birling Gap

This is a particular favourite of mine. It is a rough, rugged spot that claims a lot of tackle, but it can fish extremely well for good-sized bass. For general shore fishing, LANGREY POINT and PEVENSEY BAY are worth a visit, particularly after dark. Eastbourne Pier has long been a productive place to fish, particularly for plaice, flounders, dabs, mullet and, in the winter, cod and whiting. Like most piers Eastbourne Pier has its resident conger population, although most anglers tend to overlook these big, strong fish. I always think this is a pity. Conger, even small, 10- to 15-lb specimens, are generally a good deal larger than the average run of shore-caught fish and for sheer fighting power they can usually be relied upon to provide a few anxious minutes before they can be brought to the surface ready for gaffing.

I suppose most pier anglers fish too light for conger and so tend to regard these big eels as little more than tackle-wrecking nuisances. By using a standard outfit with a heavy rod, it is possible to fish for big eels while enjoying ordinary bottom fishing as well. A big fillet of fresh fish dropped down under the pier piles can produce some good bites and big fish. Big skelps of mackerel apeal to heavyweight bass as well as conger and more than one angler out after conger has struck at a tearaway bite only to find himself firmly attached to a specimen bass.

At CUCKMERE HAVEN, near Birling Gap, the canal-like river is often full of big mullet. River-fishing tackle and bread or ragworm bait can be used to catch these fish. Mullet fishing is never easy and these Cuckmere fish call for inexhaustible patience. Induce them to feed, however, and sport can be incredibly brisk. When I last fished this locality for mullet it took me an entire day to catch five fish. I had plenty of bites but generally missed fish on the strike. Of all sea fish, grey mullet are the most difficult fish to hook, for their habit of gently sucking the bait from the hook makes bite detection extremely difficult.

I used to use 3-lb b.s. line and a tiny quill float which took one split shot to hold it upright. With tackle as light and as delicate as this, bite detection should have been easy. Unfortunately more often than not the float would dip fractionally and the bait would be gone. Finally, by striking at the slightest movement of the float, I began to hook fish. For every fish I netted, I lost two due to the hooks pulling out. Mullet have soft lips that tear easily under pressure. Despite my losses, I was pleased with the fish I caught and felt that it had been well worth devoting the day to the Cuckmere mullet shoals.

Boat fishing in the Eastbourne area is quite good and boat trips can be arranged through local tackle shops or via the highly organised Eastbourne Angling Club on the main parade. Conger, tope, whiting, cod, mackerel, black bream, dogfish and flatfish are the main species caught in the area.

Newhaven and Seaford

Newhaven is a noted boat-fishing centre. Local charter boats operating from the harbour specialise in standard bottom-fishing trips and specialised expeditions to offshore wrecks. Catches are often very good, with cod and conger being the predominant species. Shore anglers in this area have plenty of places to choose from, but the long NEW-HAVEN JETTY is the most popular fishing platform in the area. During the summer this jetty fishes extremely well for mackerel, garfish, pouting and the occasional black bream and skate. The mackerel are caught mainly on strings of feathers cast out as far as possible and then wound back at high speed. Individual catches of fifty or more big mackerel are common and the jetty is often packed with anglers, all casting and retrieving like madmen.

During the winter months NEWHAVEN BREAKWATER can fish well for cod and whiting. These fish are normally taken on paternoster tackle baited with lugworm or strips of squid. Most of the fishing is done over the seaward wall of the breakwater. On the inshore side it is possible to catch good-sized flatfish, bass and on occasion plenty of biggish silver eels. Big bass are often found round the harbour area and some local anglers fish exclusively for them, using float tackle with live prawns as bait. Very little small-boat fishing is done in the Newhaven area due to difficult launching conditions, awkward tides, and the presence of large ships entering and leaving the quay.

Brighton

Despite its popularity as a holiday and day-triping paradise, Brighton can be a good place to fish. Local shore marks produce conger, bass, flounder, plaice, mackerel, mullet and the occasional cod, while small boats fishing offshore marks regularly come ashore with big catches of flatfish, whiting, black bream, tope and thornback skate. Boat anglers wanting information on a place to launch their own boats should contact Brighton Deep Sea Angling Club, whose HQ is in King's Road. Shore fishermen have a wide choice of beaches and rock marks available to them. Beaches like BANJO, NORFOLK and MEDINA can fish well after dark for flatfish and small bass, while BLACK ROCK, BANJO GROYNE and KING ALFRED BEACH can yield conger as well as the more normal species common to the Brighton area.

Out of the holiday season the West Pier can fish well, although sport tends to be patchy. I like small-boat fishing at Brighton for thornback skate, but to get afloat it is necessary to pick your weather conditions carefully. Most of the productive grounds lie well offshore and should conditions change for the worse, the situation can become extremely dangerous.

I remember going out on one occasion as a guest on a small boat owned by a local club member. The weather was good, the sea calm and the forecast favourable. With everything to our advantage, my host suggested a six-mile trip to an offshore mark that he felt certain would hold some good skate. Steaming out to the mark, I made my tackle ready, filleted some mackerel for bait and generally got things in order for the fishing to come. We found the mark, anchored up and soon began to get bites. To begin with we had plenty of pouting trouble. Time and again the baits would come up torn and mangled by the unwanted attentions of the pouting shoals. Abruptly these nuisances vanished, a sure sign that something big had moved into the area. Five minutes later my rod top dipped to a heavy pull and skate number one came winging reluctantly up from the depths. As I brought my fish into the boat I could see it was a female. This meant that we should now begin to catch male skate, for most thornbacks travel in small groups comprised of one female and anything up to six attendant males. The male fish tend to be smaller than the female, but even so they normally average between 7 and 10 lb, which makes them well worth catching. Sure enough, as I unhooked my fish, my host's rod began to 'knock' as a skate mouthed at the fresh strip of mackerel bait he was using. By the time I had a fresh bait on the hook he was hard into his first fish of the day, which turned out, predictably, to be a good-sized male thornback ray.

For the next hour the fish continued to bite steadily and in the excitement of good fishing we forgot to keep an eye on the weather. Suddenly a rain squall hit our small boat and we realised for the first time that the good weather of the morning had changed for the worse. With the rain came the wind and in next to no time the sea began to build up alarmingly and we realised we were in for a rough passage home. By the time we had the anchor up, conditions were far from good, and as we started the motor, the first slop of water came inboard. Six miles may not seem far on land, but on the sea it can be a long, long way from safety and we still had the problem of bringing the boat safely in through the surf on to the beach.

How much real danger was involved on this trip is hard to calculate. All I know is that a good day turned into something of a nightmare, so if you intend to fish out from Brighton, or for that matter anywhere, do not neglect to keep an eye on changing weather conditions. The best weather forecaster in the world can easily be wrong, so do not take risks. If conditions change while you are at sea, forget fishing and come back inshore to safety as soon as possible. Small-boat accidents often involve fatalities, so put safety before sport and you will not come to a great deal of harm.

An almost unbroken line of beach stretches from Brighton through HOVE and on beyond WORTHING. Practically anywhere along this beach can fish well, giving the visiting angler plenty of scope for experiment.

Littlehampton

Basically a boat-fishing port, Littlehampton is particularly famous for the quality of its black bream fishing. Although a comparatively small fish, the black bream is a vigorous fighter capable of putting up a tremendous struggle on light tackle. Black bream normally shoal in vast numbers and Littlehampton, which is the nearest port to a known black bream spawning-ground, has become the premier bream-fishing port in the British Isles. The shoals normally appear off Littlehampton during April or at the latest early May. Anglers and angling clubs book boat trips to coincide with this run of fish and to make sure of a place on a boat it is advisable to book trips months in advance.

Weighing between $1\frac{1}{2}$ and 3 lb, black bream may sound small fry to the average sea angler. Hook one of these fish on a spinning rod and 8- or 10-lb b.s. line and you will immediately appreciate why these little fish are so popular. Bite hard and fight hard—that seems to be the black bream's motto in life and on a good day when a huge shoal of bait-hungry bream are on the rampage one is almost tempted to give up fishing and rest for a while.

I have had many happy days out after the Littlehampton bream shoals, days when catches of 80 to 100 big bream have been commonplace and every angler on the boat has gone home with a bulging bag of beautiful fresh fish to show for his day out. Some anglers think bream fishing is a little too easy. Personally, I do not agree with this view. There are times when the bream shoals are so active that any angler can catch fish as fast as he can bait up, but days like this are fairly rare. The angler who can consistently come ashore with a good catch is the man who has taken the trouble to learn as much about bream and bream fishing as possible.

One of the interesting things about black bream is that they tend to constantly change their feeding levels throughout an average day's angling. To begin with they may feed on the bottom, an hour later they may well move up to the mid-water mark. This change of levels is due in part to prevailing tidal conditions but fish can be induced to rise up from the bottom by the introduction of some form of groundgait into the water. Groundbait, usually called 'shirvy' by knowledgeable bream fishermen, is an essential part of a bream-fishing expedition. Nearly always at the end of a day's bream fishing, the top boats in the port will have all used groundbait of one sort or another. I know when I go out on a bream hunt the first thing I prepare is a good supply of minced fish and squid, thickened with a mixture of bran and pilchard oil. This smelly but effective substance is packed into a fine meshed bag and tied to the anchor rope so that when the boat lies to anchor the bag hangs above the sea bed, oozing bait particles and setting up a broad smell lane that hopefully attracts and holds the attention of the hungry bream shoals.

Some anglers use this bag method and a complicated box-like bait dropper. This box which is designed to open on impact with the sea bottom is lowered down at thirty-minute intervals to dump a fresh supply of groundbait amongst the bream. I am not happy with this additional groundbait dumping. It seems to me that a heap of bait dumped on the bottom immediately washes away with the tide flow, taking most of the bream shoal with it.

As I said earlier, bream fishing is essentially a light-tackle occupation, I use a 9-ft spinning rod of the type used by freshwater pike fishermen, a small multiplier and 8-lb b.s. line. I keep terminal tackle as simple as possible, using a nylon paternoster with one hook on a long flowing nylon trace. Hook sizes depend on the bait being used, but I find a size 4 freshwater scale about right for slivers of mackerel strip, squid or worm baits. The amount of weight used should be kept to the absolute minimum with a light line whose diameter has little or no water resistance. With this I am often able to fish with weights of 1 to 2 oz irrespective of tide flow.

On the feed, black bream are bold, determined biters that snatch at the bait in a solid, decisive and totally characteristic style. Once you have experienced the bite style of black bream it is impossible to confuse the bite with that of any other species of British fish. I (and many other bream anglers) believe that black bream are attracted by a bait that moves over the sea bed, so I continually bounce my lead weight back in a search-and-find operation. This bouncing technique is simple enough to master. The rod is raised so that the lead lifts off the bottom and at the same time a yard or two of line is allowed to run off the reel. By repeating this process every minute or two, the tackle can be steadily and efficiently worked back for 100 yards or more astern of the boat.

To maintain absolute control at all times it is essential to keep a tight line between rod tip and lead weight. Slack line simply bows out in the tide, making bite detection very difficult and more often than not causing the terminal tackle to roll itself up into a badly tangled ball. Having trotted the bait back, many anglers make the mistake of retrieving at high speed. This is wrong. Sea bream will follow and take a bait that is being retrieved but only if you bring it slowly back towards the boat until you are convinced that it has risen too far off the bottom to be in any way effective. Then and only then should it be wound rapidly in, ready to start the whole trot-and-retrieve sequence again. Often when a feeding shoal is under the boat, every rod will be in action at the same instant, the skipper dashing from angler to angler with the landing net in constant use.

Although Littlehampton then is first and foremost a bream fishing port, offshore marks like KINGMERE ROCKS and the

DITCH produce good summer catches of conger, skate, tope and dogfish, while in the winter-time cod, whiting and packs of voracious spurdog are commonly encountered. Shore anglers have the choice of several local beaches and the quay walls; fishing is generally poor although it is possible to catch plaice, dabs, pouting, flounders and bass on occasion.

Bognor Regis

Like all south coast resorts. Bognor is inundated with summer visitors, consequently local beaches are best fished at night or during the winter-time when the summer crowds have dispersed. FELPHAM BEACH and PAGHAM BEACH are the best shore venues in the area. Bognor Beach is a good place to dig lugworm and soft-backed crabs can be found at Pagham Beach. Boats can be launched at Bognor and good flatfishing grounds can be found within a mile or so of the beach. Offshore marks fish well for skate, tope, conger, mackerel and flatfish and the odd cod and turbot are sometimes taken. Bognor Pier is unfortunately closed to anglers but the harbour wall at Pagham is fishable.

Portsmouth to Southsea

This is an interesting area which provides immense possibilities for shore and inshore boat fishing. The various creeks and harbours in this area offer ample opportunity to launch small boats, and for the angler who has time to explore the various stretches of available water there is every chance of finding good fishing. During the summer months the usual holiday crowds make beach fishing difficult in the area, although at nearby LANGSTONE HARBOUR and HAYLING ISLAND it is usually easy enough to tuck away in some fairly secluded spot. Portsmouth and Langstone Harbour fish well for big flounders, mullet and, provided you do not mind long, blank hours, immense bass. Bass fishing is very definitely a waiting game but for anglers who are prepared to fish the harbour entrances with big baits—whole mackerel or whole calamari squid—there is every chance of finally making contact with a bass up to or even over 10 lb.

For the more impatient anglers, flounder fishing, particularly during the winter months can be most rewarding. Few of today's anglers realise that the long-established and well-proven 'baited-spoon' technique was devised in the Langstone area by the late J. P. Gerrard whose book* on the subject of spoon fishing for flounder and to a lesser extent plaice has long been a classic work on the subject. Unfortunately this book has long been out of print, but a new edition is in preparation. It is without question the best work of its kind ever published and is invaluable to the flatfish enthusiast.

There are many theories as to why comparatively slow-moving bottom fish like flounders chase and take a bait attached to a large artificial lure. The most popular belief is that the hunting flounders see what appears to be a small flatfish making off with a large and succulent worm. Banditry is a way of life among all sea creatures and the larger fish automatically gives chase in an attempt to drag the worm away from what it believes to be a smaller fish of its own kind. I am inclined rather to believe that it is a combination of greed and curiosity that makes the adult flounder so susceptible to the spoon and bait combination. The big spoon being retrieved slowly over the muddy sea bed stirs up a cloud of silt. The hunting flounder, attracted by the disturbance, homes in on the mud trail, sees what it thinks is a small 'flattie' wrestling with a juicy worm and then, excited

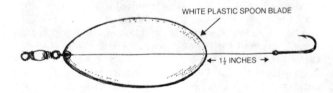

Fig. 2 Flounder spoon.

by the sight and smell of food mixed with mud-roiled water, the bigger fish simply rushes in to get what it obviously feels is an easy meal.

Whatever the reason is, the flounder spoon rig is the best

* *Sea Angling with the Baited Spoon* by Seangler (J. P. Gerrard), published by Barrie & Jenkins.

method yet devised for catching big flounders in quantity. The interesting thing about this rig is that the distance between spoon and hook is absolutely critical (see fig. 2). Without doubt, $1\frac{1}{2}$ to 2 in. is the only trail length that is acceptable to the fish. Longer or shorter trails just do not bring the results. Spoon fishing for winter flounders is an all round style of fishing. It works equally well from the shore as from a boat and any angler unable to boat fish can pick a likely shore site and use the flounder-spoon rig with every confidence of success.

Charter boats operate from all the harbours in this area. These boats specialise in fishing marks off the ISLE OF WIGHT and the NAB TOWER. Summer and winter fishing is good here with a wide variety of fish being taken. Tope and skate are the most common summer fish, although pollack, conger, bream, pouting and dogfish can be caught in quantity. During the winter cod, whiting and spurdog are the main quarry of the boat angler, with large catches of all species being recorded. Portsmouth, Emsworth and Langstone charter boats also run parties out to the famous big shark grounds off the Isle of Wight (see shark in Lymington section).

The whole of the Portsmouth area can fish well. Worm bait can be dug in many places or bought locally from tackle shops and bait dealers. For offshore work, fresh mackerel and imported squid makes the best bait.

The Solent: Southampton Water to Keyhaven

Unique in geographical layout and personal characteristics, the Solent, that apparently sheltered stretch of water between the Hampshire coast and the Isle of Wight is a fish-packed body of water capable of producing an endless stream of big fish, some of which reach record size.

Local commercial fishing boats working trawl nets in Solent waters regularly bring ashore record-breaking monkfish and tope. Anglers fishing the same areas just as regularly strike fish which make mincemeat out of heavy-boat and beach-fishing tackle—proof that monster fish of many species inhabit the murky waters of the Solent.

I have fished the Solent for over twelve years and have invariably found it to be productive, although it has its share of disadvantages, some of which are initially difficult to overcome. Strong tides and vast banks of drifting weed are the main drawbacks to Solent fishing but these hazards, coupled with comparatively shallow water, are often more than enough to put anglers off the area completely. This is a pity, for once you have learned to live with, avoid or overcome the local problems, the Solent will usually produce good catches in surprising quantities.

Lepe Beach

Although various marks inside Southampton Water fish extremely well for flounders and to a lesser extent bass, Lepe is, in my opinion, the first real beach-fishing venue in the Solent. Long noted as a bait-digging area, Lepe is a good place to shore fish for flounder, bass and the occasional big sole. STONE POINT at the eastern extremity of the beach is a favourite big bass mark and a night-fishing session here can be very rewarding indeed.

Lepe anglers tend to dig and use ragworm bait in quantity. These worms make good all-round baits, but for the big bass there is one local bait which will outcatch all the other baits yet available--cuttlefish. During May and June, enormous numbers of huge cuttlefish swarm into Solent waters to spawn and local bass stocks quickly learn to take advantage of the dead and dying cuttlefish that pile up on the Solent spawning banks. Cuttlefish are molluscs, members of the squid-octopus family and their firm, white, meaty flesh makes deadly bait. Solent anglers often deep-freeze a supply of cuttlefish during the early summer months so that they always have an ample supply of bait. For bass fishing cuttlefish should be cut into 5 to 7 in. long strips. I like to cut my baits so that each has a swallow-tailed appearance (see fig. 3). These two tails waver about in the current and

Fig. 3 Squid strip frilled out to form tentacles.

seem to make the bait more attractive to hunting fish. When cuttlefish are plentiful, it pays to obtain as many as possible, clean and cut them into bait-sized strips, pack the strips in dozens into plastic bags, and freeze each bag separately so that on each outing a bag of cut bait is ready for almost instant use.

Boat fishing off Lepe can be very good indeed. At the seaward end of Stone Point, dinghy anglers anchor for bass, while further down the Solent, in the WEST LEPE BUOY area, good tope and skate can be taken in quantity. The tope are best fished for in late April, May and early June. During these months very large female tope come into the Solent to drop their young and individual specimens to 64 lb have been caught from the West Lepe marks.

Park Shore

Once a hot-spot shore tope mark, Park Shore can still produce excellent fishing for skate, sting-ray, bass, sole and smooth hounds. The fast-moving smooth hound packs are particularly popular, for on light beach-casting outfits, these game little shark can put up a tremendous fight. Park Shore regularly produces smooth hounds of more than 20 lb. Most of these fish are caught on worm or crab bait.

Anglers who boat fish off Park Shore will be well advised to take a drop net with them. Properly baited, this net will produce an endless supply of large hermit crabs. These crabs make first-class bait and are well worth collecting in quantity.

Tanners Lane and Sowley

At Tanners Lane it is possible to launch a small boat at high tide. Various creeks and inlets at this point give direct access to the sea, but it is essential to pick high tides to get into or out of this launching area. At Sowley, a private lane leads down to the foreshore where, provided you do not mind a mud-hopping session, it is possible to slither out to a firm stance on the edge of the sea marsh.

Sowley is particularly noted for sting-ray fishing but smooth hounds, bass, conger and the odd flatfish can all be caught in this area. The sting-ray, although a dangerous fish to handle, is very popular with local and visiting anglers alike, for it gives every beach fisherman the opportunity to get to grips with a real heavyweight fighter.

Sting-ray fishing is essentially a late spring-early summer occupation. At this time of the season vast numbers of sting-ray appear in the Solent, particularly in the Sowley area. Sting-ray love mud and the sea bed off Sowley is thick black mud, packed full of all the food that big sting-ray like best.

I remember one July evening I arrived at Sowley at about six o'clock with a pair of beach-casters and three dozen big ragworms. The idea was to fish the rising tide up until after dark and my quarry was sting-ray. As evenings went, this one was ideal, no wind, overcast sky and the very definite hint of thunder in the area combined to make virtually ideal conditions for sting-ray hunting. Having the marsh to myself, I chose my position carefully, set up one rod baited up with a big king ragworm and cast out 60 yards or so to where past experience had shown was a good area for ray. With the tide only just on its way up, I took my time setting up the second rod, baited up with another snake-like worm and cast out at an angle to drop the second bait 40 yards away from where the first worm lay on the mud.

I had hardly settled the second rod into its rest when the reel ratchet on the first rod began to snarl and screech as a good fish ran off with the worm. From the wildly bucking rod tip I could see that the fish had a firm hold on the bait, so rather than strike I put the reel into gear and waited for the fish to hook itself. Sting-ray are greedy creatures which invariably swallow the bait quickly. They are also heavy, ungainly fish which can easily break a line on the strike. In past seasons I had lost a number of good fish due to breakage on strike impact and now I was content to let biting fish hook themselves. Sure enough the line came taut and the hook sank firmly into hard flesh. Almost immediately the ray broke surface in a frantic rolling plunge that showed a brief glimpse of broad wing tips through a roil of spray and flying water.

Sowley sting-ray are often hooked in very shallow water which means that they often break surface seconds after feeling the hook. This makes for exciting fishing, particularly when the big fish are on the move. I have had individual specimens at Sowley to 38 lb and other anglers have caught

40- to 45-pounders in the same area. By the look of the fish I had hooked, I reckoned it to be a 20- or possibly 25-lb fish. Now I had the job of tiring it out ready for gaffing. For a while all went well, then I heard the reel on my second rod begin to sing as another fish hurtled off seaward with the bait and hook firmly clamped into its fleshy mouth. Being by myself, I could not do anything about it, so I concentrated on beating the first fish in the hope that I could get it ashore before the second one either dragged the rod into the sea or snapped the line in its attempts to get rid of the hook.

After a ten-minute battle, I had the first fish ready for the gaff and it was painfully obvious that the second one had either shed the hook or broken the trace. Having disposed of the first fish, I retrieved the second set of gear to find the hook gone. Happy with my first sting-ray I did not worry too much about losing the other fish and, thinking that lightning never strikes in the same place twice, I tied on a new hook, re-baited both sets of tackle and cast out to approximately the same areas as before.

The bottom must have been paved with hungry sting-ray, for almost immediately both worm baits were taken and this time in succession I beached two good-sized fish. I had never experienced action like this before and deciding to take no further chances, I laid one rod aside, baited up the other and cast out. From that time on it was fish all the way, some I landed, others I lost. Not all bites resulted in hooked fish but before I ran out of bait I brought eleven good-sized rays into the gaff. Sting-ray are no good for eating purposes and having no wish to kill any of the fish I managed on each occasion to either get the hook out or cut the trace close to the ray's mouth. In this way I was able to release all the fish virtually unharmed.

Despite their ungainly shape, sting-ray are grand fighters, but they should be handled carefully. The long, serrated tail spine situated halfway up the whip-like tail is coated with a poisonous slime. A cut from this spine leaves a wicked wound that can fester. Many anglers make a habit of chopping a sting-ray's tail off before attempting to un-hook it. This is all right if the fish is going to be killed, but it is a cruel and unnecessary practice if the fish it to be returned alive. I normally pick up a bit of driftwood on the foreshore, place it over the ray's tail and hold it in place

31

with a foot while I unhook my catch. As I invariably return my sting-ray alive, I make a habit of gaffing the fish in the wing tip only. Any fish gaffed in the belly will die.

Boat fishing off the Tanners Lane–Sowley shoreline can be very productive. Sting-ray are common on the inshore marks. At Sowley, a line of posts mark the one-time submarine boom which many local anglers fish at all times. Round the piles themselves vast shoals of medium-sized bass often congregate, and spinning or trolling round the piles can be very productive. On the eastern side of the boom the water falls away into quite a deep hole. This hole can yield big fish of many kinds. Big tope are often encountered in this area and recently a monster, 64-lb monkfish was caught from the same place. Marks off the seaward end of the boom fish well for large smooth hound and good-sized thornback ray. During the winter, cod to 35 lb have been caught at this point.

For the flatfish enthusiast the Solent is generally something of a challenge. Huge sole, plaice and flounders are common throughout the length and breadth of the Solent and the Sowley area in particular. Unfortunately these fish are difficult to catch, although light tackle anglers have caught many 3-lb plus sole and 4-lb to 6-lb plaice from these grounds.

The Solent is in fact a good all-round area. These days most anglers tend to overlook its fine potential and the anglers who do fish its murky waters try where possible to keep their big catches out of the angling newspapers. Fished on a regular basis, however, the Solent from Southampton Water to Hurst Castle can produce big fish of many kinds in large numbers. It is not the easiest stretch of water to fish but for any angler willing to learn, the Solent is something of a south coast El Dorado.

Lymington to Poole

From the shore- and boat-fishing point of view, the section of Hampshire and Dorset coastline that lies between Lymington and Poole provides a wealth of often rich and varied fishing. Taken on a year-round basis the fishing in this area is good provided you learn to switch styles of angling and choice of venue to suit the changing seasons

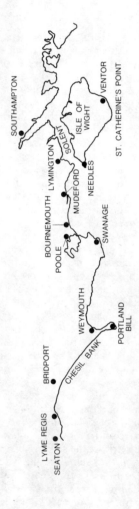

and the mood of the fish you hope to catch. Like most areas this extensive section of coastline can have its off period.

Lymington and Keyhaven

Small-boat anglers fishing in the creeks that filter off the Lymington River estuary can often catch good bags of bass during the summer-time, and big hauls of plump flounder during the cold winter months. Pylwell Creek is a good place to try and the saltwater lake that opens up beyond the new marina provides good sport.

At the actual river mouth to the right or left of the navigable channel fishing can be very good indeed. During the months of February, March and April I do a great deal of small-boat fishing in this area with bass as my main quarry. Despite the fact that the fish average only 2 to 4 lb, they put up a great fight on light tackle and amply repay the effort involved. Practically any point between Lymington River mouth and the entrance to Keyhaven will yield good bass catches between February and April. I use a light spinning rod, fixed-spool reel and 8-lb line for this inshore bass fishing. Mostly the fish in this area are caught in less than 10 ft of water and under most circumstances it is possible to fish with weights of $\frac{1}{2}$ oz or $\frac{3}{4}$ oz. The idea is to anchor the boat in a suitable locality, cast uptide of the boat and allow the tackle to roll slowly across the sea bed until it finally comes to rest astern of the boat. This rolling leger technique is particularly effective for bass and many bites occur as the bait is rolling across the sea bed.

Bass are natural predators which can be attracted to a worm bait by attaching a tiny spoon 6 in. up the line from the bait. This spoon acts in two ways. First it twinkles and flashes attractively as the baited tackle rolls steadily over the sea bed, then when the tackle is being retrieved in preparation for another cast, it spins rapidly to attract fish by both visual impact and vibration waves. Many bites will occur during the retrieve, the striking fish normally hooking themselves firmly as they slam into the bait.

The best spinner to use is the smallest Mepps spoon. This is usually sold complete with treble hook. To convert the spoon into an attractor lure, this hook should be removed to allow a 6 in. nylon hook-length to be attached to the

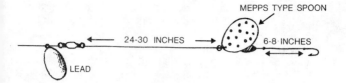

Fig. 4   Inshore bass rig.

lower eye of the spoon mount (see fig 4). Use rag or
lugworm as bait. This tiny rig is a local device but the basic
principle could easily be adapted for use in any bass fishing
area.

Bass apart, this area can fish well for flounders, plaice,
small skate, surprisingly heavy conger and, in the winter,
the occasional cod. Further out in the Solent good mixed
fishing is within easy reach, although strong tides and drifting weed can make angling difficult.

From Lymington round to Keyhaven miles of sea wall
fronting directly on to tidal creeks and saltwater inlets give
the shore angler ample scope to pick and choose good fishing spots. Bass are plentiful throughout the summer months
and small to medium specimens make up the major part of
all catches. From October through to March these sea walls
also fish extremely well for flounders. Local clubs hold
regular flounder festivals in this locality and individual
catches are often high. Local experts favour a slowly-
retrieved baited spoon for flounder fishing, although good
catches can be made on leger tackle as well. Unfortunately
green shore crabs can make a real nuisance of themselves
here which is one reason the local specialists like to keep
their baits on the move.

Hurst Castle to Milford-on-Sea

From Milford-on-Sea a long shingle bank juts firmly out
into the Solent. On the seaward end, close to Hurst Castle
and its lighthouse, beach anglers can cast directly out into
extremely deep water. Reachable either by a long, hard walk
over heavy shingle, or during the summer months by ferry
from Keyhaven, Hurst Castle fishes extremely well.

On the Solent side of the shingle bank, sheltered from the

prevailing south-west winds, there is good flatfishing ground. Flounders, plaice, dabs and bass can all be caught from this side of the shingle spit but the best fishing of all is to be found round the head of the bank. At Hurst Castle the Solent narrows abruptly so that all the tides are channelled into one bottleneck of water. This has scooped out a vast hole in the sea bed which is over 300 feet deep in places. Of course, the beach itself does not fall away directly into such deep water, but a cast of 60 to 100 yards will drop the bait into very deep water indeed.

Because of these unique geographical features, Hurst shingle bank is a place where the unexpected often occurs. Several years ago, for example, a beach angler hooked and finally beached a magnificent 69-lb common skate. Big conger can also be caught from the deep water at the head of the bank and during the winter months cod and good-sized whiting are often caught. Summer anglers out after mackerel regularly fish this area, for the strong tides and deep water bring the mackerel shoals into easy casting range of the beach. The normal technique when the mackerel are in is to use a beach-casting outfit to throw out a set of six gaudy mackerel feathers. These are then retrieved at high speed and big catches of prime mackerel are made.

The whole of the Milford shingle bank is fishable and any point along the mile or so of steep shingle can provide good fishing. Bass are particularly prolific in this area, but thornback skate, pouting and sole can also be taken. The shingle bank provides ample scope for the light-tackle man to try his luck with a spinning outfit; big bass often feed within easy range of the bank and in past seasons local anglers using Toby spoons or similar lures have caught bass of over 10 lb.

Milford-on-Sea to Highcliffe

Basically a continuation of the same beach, the shoreline that stretches between Milford and Highcliffe is well worth fishing. At Milford beach, anglers fishing during the late evening catch sole, plaice, thornback skate, pouting and bass. During August and September sole fishing is particularly good, but, like most flatfish, sole tend to be nocturnal feeders and to get the best results it pays to fish late evenings or through the night. Even big sole have small mouths and it is advisable to use rag or lugworm bait on long-shanked, narrow-gape size 1 or 2 flatfish hooks.

Sixty or more yards off Milford Beach a reef of sand and shingle reaches almost to the surface. On the shoreward side of this natural breakwater, a deep gully has formed. A bait dropped into this gully stands more chance of attracting fish than one cast beyond it. At TADDIFORD GAP the water is very shallow and the breaking waves create an ideal feeding area for bass. On calm days Taddiford can also produce flatfish but most anglers fish this section of coastline primarily for bass.

Beyond Taddiford, the next easily accessible beach area is at BARTON. A longish walk over the golf course will bring you to BECTON BUNNY where a stream has cut through the cliffs to form a natural gorge. The beach at this point is extremely rocky and a sewer pipe empties out some 80 yards offshore. The combination of inflowing fresh water and sewerage discharge seems to be highly attractive to bass and sole and local anglers regularly make good catches in this area.

Despite its featureless appearance, Barton Beach is well worth fishing, for it is on this beach that many double-figure bass have been caught. Most of these fish have ranged in size from 10 to 13 lb, but bigger specimens have been hooked and lost. Most of the big bass caught at Barton have fallen to leger tackle baited with half a mackerel or a whole small pouting. Ragworm and squid is also worth trying.

STEAMER POINT at Highcliffe is another good big-bass venue. I have fished this point on many occasions and find that the bass fishing is best during September and October. I normally fish at night and all the bass I have caught have been taken on squid bait. During the winter months, cod can also be caught from this point. Little or no inshore dinghy fishing is done in this area, because there are no launching facilities available from Milford to Christchurch.

Christchurch Harbour and Mudeford

At Mudeford the combined estuaries of the Hampshire Avon and Dorset Stour flow out to sea through a remarkably narrow estuary mouth. The combined force of two heavy rivers meeting the sea causes a strong tidal flow and the 'run' at Mudeford has long been noted as a dangerous piece of water. Anglers using small boats in this area are well advised to confine their fishing activities to the miles of protected water inside Christchurch Harbour. This is no real handicap, for bass, mullet and flounders abound within the confines of the harbour and its adjacent saltwater creeks. Grey mullet are particularly common and the favourite local method is to spin for these elusive fish using a totally localised baited-spoon rig (see fig. 5).

Mullet do not usually chase, let alone strike at, a spinner. Christchurch mullet, however, find the flashing appeal of a tiny spoon irresistible and provided the single hook is baited with a tiny scrap of ragworm, the fish will chase and snatch at the spoon until they become firmly hooked. Mullet spinning here is essentially a light tackle sport. Trout spinning rods and lines in the 3- to 5-lb b.s. range are ample. Big mullet hooked on tackle of this calibre are more than capable of putting up an incredible battle when hooked. More important still, the use of light lines and flexible rods cuts down fish loss to an acceptable level. This is an important factor, for the soft-mouthed grey mullet are quick to tear off a hook if undue pressure is exerted during the initial stages of the fight.

Mullet can also be caught on float tackle baited with bread or harbour ragworm. Once again this is a light-tackle sport and most local experts use roach-style tackle. The

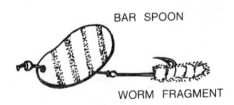

BAR SPOON

WORM FRAGMENT

Fig. 5 Baited spoon for mullet. Approximately natural size.

technique is to trot the baited hook down alongside the main flow of river water. The mullet shoals tend to gather just out of the main current. By using plenty of bread-based groundbait it does not take long to get the fish feeding avidly. Bass and flounders are usually taken on leger tackle baited with ragworm.

Shore anglers fishing at STANPIT often catch big bass and good-sized flounders on leger tackle. The quay wall at Mudeford is worth fishing, particularly after dark when bass, flounders and the occasional conger eel can be caught. Several years ago an angler fishing from this wall caught a huge torpedo ray. AVON BEACH close to Mudeford Harbour is a good spot to try for flatfish and small bass, and fishes best after dark.

Hengistbury Head

Hengistbury Head is a favourite shore-fishing resort with local sea-angling clubs. Regular beach-fishing competitions are held in this area and fair catches of mixed bass, flatfish and pouting are commonly made. A great attraction is the long groyne that juts out to sea. By walking out on this groyne it is possible to fish into quite deep water. For the angler interested in big fish, the groyne can fish fairly well for conger eels and, in the winter, the occasional cod. Bass, mullet, small wrasse and flatfish can also be caught along the entire length of the groyne.

Southbourne

The pier at Southbourne fishes consistently well for flatfish, bass, mullet, mackerel, garfish and the occasional winter cod. Most of the fish are caught by casting well out from the pier. Big mullet, bass and the odd fair-sized conger can be caught round the pier piles and it does not do to concentrate entirely on distance casting.

Southbourne's beaches, like most of the beaches in the area, tend to be rather featureless but they do fish well for flatfish and school bass. For the offshore angler, SOUTH-BOURNE ROUGH is well worth a try. This is an area of rough ground situated a mile or so off the pier. During the summer the rough is a good mark for bream, pouting, conger and skate. Big tope can also be encountered and more than one 50-lb plus specimen has been caught off Southbourne. During the winter months, the rough is a good place to catch cod. Fish to 42 lb have been caught in this area and the average size of rod-caught cod is 16 to 20 lb—good fish by any standards. These big cod mainly fall to whole imported Californian squid.

Bournemouth

Bournemouth Pier is the big attraction with local and visiting anglers. This pier often fishes extremely well for flatfish and bass. Float fishing with mackerel-strip bait also produces big catches of mackerel and garfish during the summer months. Occasionally catches of black bream are made, but these fish cannot be relied on to appear round the pier on a regular basis. Rowing boats can be hired from the adjacent beach and as small-boat fishing a mile or so off-shore can be very good, these are well worth considering.

Bournemouth Bay is particularly good for plaice fishing, the technique being to drift with the tide using a baited-spoon or leger rig to attract the fish. Over-fishing by commercial boats has rather decimated the once immense stocks of prime plaice. Despite this, it is usually possible to catch a few good fish on each outing—I have had up to twenty nice 1- to $2\frac{1}{2}$-lb fish in a single session.

During the summer months, daytime fishing from Bournemouth Beach is practically impossible. After dark, however, the beaches are clear of bathers and can be used for fishing purposes. Flatfish and bass are the only two types of fish you can expect on a regular basis while beach fishing in this area and as a rule most of the fish caught tend to be on the small side.

Poole Harbour

Poole Harbour, with its 96 square miles of coastline, is the second largest natural harbour in the world and as such it is bound to attract anglers. At one time plaice were the favourite local species and in past years many huge plaice were caught from various marks round BROWNSEA ISLAND. Unfortunately over-fishing by anglers and commercial fishermen seems to have virtually wiped out big plaice stocks, although the odd outsized fish can still be caught.

Plaice aside, Poole Harbour is still something of an angler's paradise. Anyone who reads the popular angling press will soon realise that the harbour and its adjacent fishing grounds continually makes news with big fish and big catches. Anglers fishing the quay at Poole catch flounders, small plaice and good bass. At HAMWORTHY, light leger and spinning tackle regularly accounts for big bass and at the mouth of Poole Harbour good catches of small bass and flatfish are commonplace. From the boat-angling point of view, anywhere in the harbour is capable of producing good fishing, although most anglers concentrate on marks round Brownsea Island where flatfish, bass, conger and pouting can be caught. Bass fishing around the mouth of Poole Harbour can provide exciting fishing.

Although it is possible to fish this area from small boats, strong tides can make the harbour entrance very dangerous to the novice boatman or the man without local knowledge. For this reason, I would suggest that it is wise to book trips on established charter fishing boats whose skippers know the area well. Offshore marks are good for skate, tope, conger, black bream and a variety of lesser species. Light-tackle bass enthusiasts can arrange trips to the Training Bank grounds which in recent seasons have produced immense catches of huge bass. Most of these fish are caught on rubber eels or driftlined natural baits. Poole and Bournemouth are well endowed with tackle shops and lugworm can be dug at SANDBANKS.

Isle of Wight

Like most islands the Isle of Wight is more than capable of providing a wide variety of good fishing. Once famous as a shark-fishing centre the island has a local reputation for producing big fish from shore stations and inshore boat fishing marks as well.

Beach fishing is good right round the island. Favourite marks being ALUM BAY, BROOK and CHALE beaches, and SANDOWN BAY. Bass, conger, skate and even big monkfish can be caught at Brook and Chale. The other beaches produce mainly bass and flatfish.

Pier anglers will be well advised to head for the mile-long pier at RYDE, or the piers at VENTNOR or SHANKLIN. Flatfish, mackerel and big mullet are the main fish caught by pier anglers, but bass and conger eel can also be taken.

Small-boat fishing is good right round the island. Tides can, however, be very strong indeed so care must be taken to keep out of the main tidal streams. Much of the island's coastline is very exposed to prevailing winds so a weather eye should be kept open at all times. At the slightest sign of an increase in wind strength it pays to forget fishing and come ashore as quickly as possible.

Channel Islands

Good shore fishing can be found right round the Channel Islands with bass, mullet and flatfish as the main quarry. With a spring tide rise and fall at more than 40 feet it pays to keep an eye on the tide. It is only too easy to become cut off by a fast advancing tide particularly when the fishing is good. For the surf fishing enthusiast the Guernsey beaches of COBO, VAZON and GRANDES ROCQUES are ideal. ST OWEN'S BAY on Jersey can also be productive. In many areas black bream can be caught from rocks and breakwaters. When I last fished off Jersey ST CATHERINE'S BREAKWATER and BOULEY BAY were the favourite black bream areas. L'ANCRESSE BAY on Guernsey also produces black bream.

Scilly Islands

Largely untouched, the Scillies are more than capable of providing first-class fishing for a wide variety of fish. Wrasse, bass, conger, dogfish, mullet, flatfish and pollack can be caught at almost any point round the islands, and for the angler who wants to get away and explore a practically virgin area, the Scilly Islands are the place to head for.

CHAPTER 3

The West Country Coast

Swanage to Seaton

Beyond Poole the coastline changes character considerably. High cliffs interspersed with small sheltered beaches provide ample scope for the shore and dinghy angler alike, with a wide variety of fish available from most marks.

Beyond the cliffs of STUDLAND, Swanage Bay opens up to provide a wealth of good fishing. Shore anglers fishing this area can expect to catch bass, conger, pouting, dab, plaice and mullet. Swanage Pier can fish well at times, particularly for mullet and mackerel. Swanage Bay itself is good for boat fishing. Small-boat anglers fishing this bay catch thornback ray, tope, pollack, conger, pouting, dogfish, various flatfish, bass and black bream. During May and June, rock marks in the bay are often inundated with shoals of big black bream. Most of these fish are caught in the vicinity of Studland Bay and OLD HARRY ROCKS. Individual catches of forty or more bream in a tide are common.

The best bait in this area seems to be ragworm or fish and squid strip baits. Heavyweight tope often come into Swanage Bay and many anglers boat fishing in the bay have been smashed up by these hard-fighting little sharks which can weigh up to 50 lb.

Kimmeridge

Anglers fishing this stretch of the Dorset coastline often bypass some tremendous fishing areas which lie directly between Swanage and Weymouth. Kimmeridge is a typical example of an overlooked fishing ground. Situated some five miles from Corfe Village, Kimmeridge Bay is controlled by a local estate which charges a toll fee for parking and fishing. The bay consists of numerous ledges of flat rock which run straight out from the beach. At first sight these ledges and the comparatively shallow water of the bay appears to offer little opportunity for angling. Examine any of the local rock pools, however, and you will quickly discover that the bay is alive with shellfish, shrimps, prawns, crabs and tiny rock fish. It is a natural, well-stocked larder which is more than capable of providing large predatory fish with an ample and easily obtainable supply of live food.

Tope, conger, bass, pollack and some monster mullet use Kimmeridge Bay as a feeding ground and anglers who are prepared to put in time and thought can really get to grips with some big fish in this shallow and sheltered bay. Local bass specialists have devised and developed an interesting style of angling specifically for fishing round the Kimmeridge rock ledges. Conventional bottom fishing usually leads to lost tackle, so in an attempt to minimise tackle losses, local anglers have taken to using spinning tackle and floating-plug-style baits (see fig. 6). Plug baits originated in the U.S.A. but have long been popular in this country for pike and salmon fishing. Plugs come in a wide variety of sizes, shapes and weights. For fishing the Kimmeridge ledges, however,

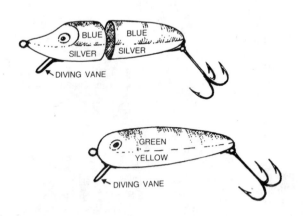

Fig. 6 Plug baits. To avoid continual snagging only one set of treble hooks should be used.

the local specialists use only the lightweight floating-style plug. This lure, as its name suggests, floats on the surface until retrieved. Then and only then does it duck under the water to sidle seductively along, simulating the movement of a sick or damaged fish. The beauty of this buoyant bait is that it can be worked over or round submerged obstructions. At Kimmeridge, for example, the plug is cast out into open water well beyond the rock ledges, then worked back steadily until it reaches the sunken rock, then the angler stops winding in line and the plug immediately surfaces. Once in sight it can be worked over the top of the rock until the next section of open water is reached. In this way the bait can cover the maximum amount of fishable water with the minimum possibility of getting lost in the process.

Apart from bass, Kimmeridge will yield big tope and conger eels. For both species it pays to fish the extremities of the bay where it is possible to cast out into comparatively deep water. Boat fishing off Kimmeridge can be very good indeed. The whole area is alive with fish of many kinds, including a plentiful supply of beautiful, big black bream. Apart from these bream, which tend to be fussy feeders, Kimmeridge is the sort of place where big baits pay off handsomely. In my experience, a whole mackerel or pouting is more likely to catch fish than a fillet or fish strip bait. Tope, conger and good-sized skate abound in this area and all three tend to prefer one big meal rather than a whole series of snacks.

There is also the chance of a bonus in the shape of a big succulent turbot. More than one 20-lb turbot has been caught on the marks off Kimmeridge Bay and I think that if anyone actually set out to fish hard for this species, results might be spectacular.

CHAPMAN'S POOL and DURDLE DOOR are other shore venues in this area which could easily repay a little effort and exploration. At Chapman's Pool, night fishing for big bass using a plain running leger baited with squid or half a mackerel can produce fish to 10 lb or more. There is also the chance of getting a good conger in the same way. Durdle Door is also a big-fish venue which can produce the odd surprise catch. I remember fishing this spot for a whole night without even a bite to show for my effort, then, just as dawn broke, a shoal of magnificent black bream came on the feed and in less than an hour I beached eleven really hefty specimens. Big wrasse are a possibility all along this coast and by fishing from the rocks with prawn or ragworm bait it is often possible to catch some fair specimen ballan wrasse.

Weymouth

Long established as a top boat-fishing site, Weymouth and its surrounding area is also something of a shore-angler's paradise. Always a popular holiday resort, Weymouth's town beach is virtually unfishable during the summer months, but the stone pier at the harbour mouth is well worth trying, particularly for conger eels. Float fishing from the pier head sometimes produces good mixed bags of fish, mackerel and pollack being the main species encountered.

Rock-fishing enthusiasts should head for nearby PORTLAND. The whole area round Portland is worth fishing, although in many places the climb down to water level is only for those with a fine disregard for personal safety and a very good head for heights. For the less adventurous, there are plenty of places round the PORTLAND LIGHTHOUSE which provide easy-to-get-at, safe casting positions. The flat ledge adjacent to PULPIT ROCK is a typical and popular example of the kind of fishing station I mean. This broad, easily accessible ledge allows the angler to float or bottom fish in absolute comfort and yet still stand every chance of catching some good-sized fish. This is a favourite venue with local anglers and visitors alike. Close to a good car park, easy to walk to and simple to fish, Pulpit Rock and its adjoining ledge is as good a place to start as any round Portland. Bass, conger, wrasse and pollack are the mainstay of Portland's rock fishing. Catch a bass in this area and the chances are it will be a big hefty 6-, 8- or even 10-lb specimen. Wrasse, too, grow to good sizes here and of course there are the resident conger, some of which weigh well over 40 lb: odd 50-lb plus conger are still caught by shore anglers and even bigger fish are known to exist.

Mackerel, garfish, bull huss and mullet can be caught all round PORTLAND BILL. It was this area that produced the long-standing British mullet record and, as most of the regular local anglers will tell you, monster mullet still exist round the cliffs and gullies of Portland. These giants are there in vast numbers but, like most grey mullet, very difficult fish to catch. Extremely shy at the best of times, Portland mullet take fright at the slightest indication of danger and to be successful it is essential to adopt the fine and far-off tactics practised by freshwater anglers. Big mullet are tackle-shy and to fish for these grey ghosts with conventional sea-fishing tackle is generally a total waste of time and effort.

A trotting rod, fixed-spool reel loaded wth 3- or 4-lb b.s. line is about the ideal combination for these rock mullet. Most Portland mullet fall to float-fished bread-paste bait on a size 8–10 freshwater-scale hook. Pre-baiting is essential for rock-haunting mullet shoals. This can be done in a variety of ways. One specialist I know pre-baits by ramming fistfuls of mashed bread into rock crevices at low tide. As the tide rises to cover the rocks and the crevices, the flow of the water continually loosens the bread mix so that a constant stream of bait particles is released. The browsing mullet shoals home-in on this stream of groundbait until, with luck, they become concentrated in one small area. Whichever way you go about it, ground baiting is an essential part of normal mullet fishing. The angler who neglects this aspect of his fishing deserves what he gets, which is usually next to nothing.

Between Portland and Weymouth the road passes over a narrow neck of water known as the Fleet. This runs up behind CHESIL BEACH and is a good place for flatfish and the occasional monster bass. In periods of rough weather, when beach and rock fishing is virtually impossible, the Fleet provides comfortable, often rewarding fishing.

Chesil Bank

Eighteen miles of steep-to shingle makes up the famed Chesil Bank. A long-established shore angling hot-spot, the bank can produce a wide variety of fish, some of which grow to a vast size. This is one of the few beaches in the British Isles where you might well hook a shark. More than one unfortunate angler has suddenly found himself well attached to a big thresher shark and porbeagle shark have been known to come well within casting range.

Chesil Bank is a year-round venue; conger, skate, tope, flatfish and mackerel make up the bulk of the summer catches, while winter anglers find big cod, whiting and hefty spurdog. Chesil Bank once held the British spurdog record with a magnificent 16-lb 1-oz specimen. This record stood for many years until finally a 20-pounder was caught by a boat angler fishing off the Isle of Wight.

It would never surprise me to find that yet another record-breaking spurdog has been caught off Chesil Bank. for during the winter months immense packs of big spurdog rove the entire length of this vast beach. Summer or winter, Chesil Beach is essentially a big fish site. Knowledgeable anglers invariably fish here with fairly heavy tackle and big baits. Huge tope and conger are commonly hooked along the beach and monster monkfish are very occasionally encountered.

Big fish prey on small fish and for the angler who likes to fish light for flatfish or bass, Chesil Bank has much to offer. Night fishing produces the best results, but the beach can fish well during the daytime, particularly after a storm when the water is coloured by clouds of disturbed sand. At times like this, bass and flatfish often bite freely and the angler who is prepared to use big baits and wait patiently for a bite can often finish up the day with a nice big thornback ray or two to show for his efforts.

Practically any section of Chesil Beach is worth fishing, although it is difficult to gain access to much of the beach. Favourite, easily-reached venues like SEATOWN, EYPE, ABBOTSBURY, BURTON BRADSTOCK and WEST BEXINGTON are often heavily fished. During the summer months Chesil Bank Beach is noted for its productive mackerel fishing. Vast shoals of these fast-moving fish sweep right inshore in search of whitebait and many anglers fish the bank specifically for mackerel.

However, Chesil Bank mackerel fishing is hardly a sporting affair. Most anglers use heavy beach-casters, a big 6- to 8-oz lead and a string of six or more feathers to take mackerel in quantity. The technique is simple. You either wait patiently for signs of a shoal working small fish and then cast directly beyond the shoal to bring the feathers back through the food-mad mackerel, or you simply work on the constant cast-and-retrieve technique until you make contact with a passing mackerel shoal. This is production-line fishing, the object being to catch as many mackerel as possible, and sport does not enter into it at all. Naturally, the thrill of catching mackerel six at a time holds an appeal for the novice sea angler, but this enjoyment soon begins to pall.

Whenever I fish Chesil Bank, I take a light-spinning rod, fixed-spool reel and heavy Abu Costa spoon with me. I keep this outfit permanently at the ready so that whenever a mackerel pack puts in an appearance, I can swing straight into action. By taking the fish singly on light tackle I am able to enjoy mackerel fishing as a sporting proposition, rather than a mass-slaughter operation. Mackerel are more than capable of putting up a magnificent fight, and on the spinning gear that I use, each fish can be relied upon to give incredible sport.

The coastline at BRIDPORT is really part of the Chesil Bank, but it is possible to fish from the walls of West Bay harbour. This again is a good place for mackerel and all the other species of fish that frequent Chesil Bank.

It is possible to launch small boats at many points along Chesil Bank. Dinghy fishermen do very well in this area, for by using a boat it is possible to fish many highly productive marks which, while not far offshore, are still well beyond casting range of the beach. By boat fishing it is possible to catch pollack, black bream and one or two other species of fish which are rarely encountered by anglers fishing from the Chesil Bank. Great care should be taken when boat fishing at any point off Chesil, for this is an exposed coastline which can become extremely dangerous very quickly. Keep an eye on the weather and wind strength and do not take silly chances and you will not come to much harm. Ignore the signs and you could easily be in serious, or even fatal, trouble very quickly.

Lyme Regis

Although the harbour at Lyme Regis tends to dry out at low water, adjacent beaches are fishable at most states of the tide. This entire area is good for bass fishing. CHURCH BEACH, CHURCH CLIFF BEACH and WESTERN BEACH are the favourite local venues. They produce conger, bass, skate, wrasse, flatfish, mullet and the occasional good-sized tope. Boat fishing in Lyme Bay is generally quite good, skate being extremely common at most times of the year.

Seaton

Noted for its big bass, Seaton Beach is well worth a visit. One of the best places to fish is at the estuary of the RIVER AXE. This is often thick with shoaling mullet and anyone who likes mullet fishing will be well advised to try their luck here. Bass, and flatfish and mullet also run into this narrow waterway and at various times some pretty hefty bass have been caught in this area. I once lived in Seaton and at that time I concentrated on bass fishing in the hope of making contact with a 10-lb specimen. Often I fished at night to avoid the holiday crowds and on many occasions my night-fishing sessions paid off.

I remember one dark autumn night when a fresh breeze had whipped up a good surf. The tide was coming in and at the river mouth the force of the meeting waters had created a sort of boiling cauldron of white water. While live sand-eels are very good, my favourite big bass bait at that time was a mackerel head cut so that the guts of the fish were left attached. This bait had accounted for many good bass in the past sessions and on this night, with conditions near perfect, I had high hopes of making contact with a bigger-than-average specimen.

Casting out to drop the bait on the edge of the white water, I balanced the rod carefully in my hands and settled back to await a bite. Bass fishing is never a speedy business but I like to hold the rod at all times rather than use a rod rest, for when a bass does bite I like to be able to take positive action at the first indication that a fish has picked up the bait. I waited thirty minutes, then had a bait check to see if the mackerel head had been mauled about by shore crabs. It had not, so I cast out to approximately the same position and settled back again to wait for a feeding fish to come on the scene.

Twenty minutes later it happened. The rod tip twitched slightly as a fish plucked gently at the bait. Wise in the ways of feeding bass, I dropped the rod tip slightly to give slack line. Seconds later the fish made up its mind. One moment nothing, the next a screaming, tearing run which ripped line at incredible speed off the protesting reel. Slamming the rod hard back, I set the big 6–0 hook solidly and for the first time felt the weight of the fish as it went over in a rolling lunge that again had the tortured reel screeching its steel throat out. Alone in the dark, on a deserted beach, I knew the full thrill of making solid contact with one of the world's great fighting fish. With the long rod bent almost double, giving and gaining line, I fought it out with a fish that obviously knew every line-breaking trick in the book. Time and again it doubled back on its tracks, leaving me to think it was gone. Seconds later the slack line would snap taut and again I would be struggling to control the speed and temper of the bass.

Finally it was over. The long high-speed runs had finished, now the fish was giving line quickly, wagging its blunt head slowly from side to side, circling wearily. Finally I waded into the surf to pick the beaten fish up by its sharp gill plates. To my eye it looked every inch a ten-pounder, but the scales proved me wrong by showing a weight of 9 lb 10 oz. By a scant 6 oz I had missed my long-hoped-for 10-lb Seaton beach bass.

So far I have never had a better bass than this from Seaton, but I know other anglers who have had double-figure specimens and there are still plenty of big bass along this section of coastline, so, who knows, I may still achieve my ambition to get that 10-lb Seaton beach bass.

Boat fishing off Seaton is basically good. Skate, conger, bream, dogfish, pollack, mackerel and garfish are plentiful. This is quite a good area to dinghy fish, although the rather steep-to shingle beach can make launching and beaching a boat difficult in all but calm seas.

Exmouth to Plymouth

Most anglers who visit this section of the South Devon coastline automatically gravitate towards Brixham. During the past decade Brixham has become a sort of Mecca for boat fishermen from all over the British Isles and also from the Continent. Most of these anglers come for the wreck-fishing and seldom does a week pass without Brixham-based boats bringing in mammoth catches of monster conger, ling, pollack and coalfish. Due to the amount of publicity given to these huge catches, few anglers realise that the south coast of Devon can offer a wide variety of good shore and inshore fishing. I suppose this is understandable when one sees the photographs of the kind of fish brought in by the

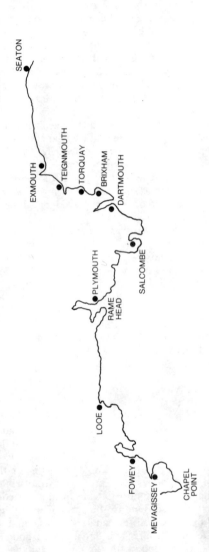

deep-sea boats. Sixty-pound conger are commonplace and pollack of 18 lb or so are reckoned to be little more than average catches.

In the face of this sort of fishing, beach-casting, rock fishing and small-boat fishing seem to be very dull forms of angling. In fact this whole stretch of rugged coastline is more than capable of giving good fishing, albeit with mini-monsters. Big wrasse and bass abound and there are many places where the shore and inshore dinghy fishermen can expect to catch conger eels of up to and possibly just over 40 lb. A fish of this size may look small beside a 60- or 80-lb wreck-caught eel but the fact remains that a 40-lb conger is a good, big fish by any normal standards and in any other place an inshore eel of this size would be recognised as the catch of a lifetime. Do not make the mistake of under-estimating or in any way of overlooking the fine fishing potential of this rich and varied coastline.

Exmouth

Although a popular holiday resort, Exmouth has good fishing. School bass and flounders are very common in this area, particularly from BULL HILL BANK and SHELLEY GUT. ORCOMBE POINT BEACH and ROCKS provide good mixed fishing for conger, bass, wrasse, flatfish, dogfish and the very occasional tope. Night fishing from the old jetty and Exmouth Pier can provide good sport, particularly with small conger eels. Dangerous tides make small-boat fishing difficult, although offshore marks can produce good mixed catches.

Teignmouth

This is basically a flatfish and bass area. Local anglers fish the river a great deal using live sand-eels as bass bait and ragworm for flatfish. Small-boat fishing within the river mouth can produce splendid catches of big plaice and medium-sized bass. Grey mullet are also very common in the river, although few anglers fish for them. During the winter months good catches of big flounders can be made from marks in the river. A rolling leger or baited spoon is the best terminal rig to use for these fish.

Torquay

Long established as a holiday playground, Torquay is also famous for the quality of its shore fishing. Probably the most noted mark in the Torquay area is HOPE'S NOSE, a peninsular which can be reached via the Marine Drive. Hope's Nose is one of those all-round marks which constantly produces surprise catches. In past seasons the Nose has produced award-winning wrasse, plaice, conger, bass and even oddities like angler fish. It is also a favourite mackerel-fishing station and can usually be relied upon to produce good bags of prime mackerel to float and spinning tackle. Anglers who have plenty of time and patience to spare will be well advised to try for grey mullet round the Nose, for at times huge shoals come into this area to feed.

Apart from Hope's Nose, WATCOMBE, ANSTEY'S COVE and ABBEY SANDS are well worth fishing. All are capable of producing mixed fishing, although Hope's Nose is by far the best shore station in the area. Torquay Harbour provides plenty of pier-jetty fishing. These spots are good for flatfish, mackerel, garfish, bass, mullet and fair-sized conger eels.

Dinghy fishing off Torquay is generally good.

Brixham

Quite apart from the excellence of its offshore boat-fishing grounds, Brixham yields good catches to the shore and inshore dinghy angler. The most popular shore-fishing venue is the breakwater. This spot is often used for club and inter-club competitions, many of which are won by high individual bags of good-sized fish. Big wrasse are often caught from the breakwater in quantity and at one time many competitions were won with this species.

During the summer months the holiday crowds make most of the local beaches unfishable. At night, however, most beaches fish well for a wide variety of species.

Night-fishing sessions on the breakwater invariably produce some fair catches of conger and the usual spate of monster-conger stories. In most cases these stories are factual. Some very big eels are known to frequent the breakwater area and more often than not these bigger-than-average fish manage to smash up the tackle of any angler fortunate—or unfortunate—enough to hook them. Quite apart from wrasse and conger, the breakwater also produces pouting, mackerel, mullet, garfish, pollack and the usual flatfish.

Anglers wishing to boat fish can either launch their own craft or hire small boats by the hour, half-day or day from the beach at ST MARY'S BAY. Small-boat fishing in the Brixham area is good. Quite apart from the species encountered by the shore angler, it is possible to catch tope, monkfish, skate and even the odd cod while inshore-boat fishing. A running leger employing one or at the most two hooks is the best terminal rig to use.

There are some very hefty wrasse to be had in the Brixham area and the best way of catching these big fish it to employ the one bait that most big wrasse just cannot refuse—prawn. By using a drop net baited with a bit of smelly fish it is usually possible to catch a good supply of biggish prawns and these used on float or paternoster tackle can usually be relied upon to produce plenty of bites and action when other baits fail to interest the wrasse shoals.

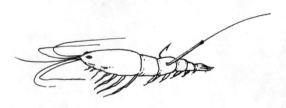

Fig. 7   Hooking a prawn.

The best place to find prawns in quantity is round the soft weed that grows on quay walls. A baited drop net lowered down beside this weed will usually catch prawns in quantity. Prawns should be used alive. The best way to hook a prawn is through one of the tail segments (see fig. 7). A bait hooked in this way will stay on the hook during casting and remain lively for a considerable period of time. Prawns are a fragile bait and wrasse are adept at nipping them off the hook. To overcome this problem it is essential to strike at the slightest indication of a bite. Wait for the bite to develop and you will simply lose the bait.

Dartmouth

Now primarily a wreck-fishing centre, Dartmouth is also capable of producing good shore and inshore boat fishing as well. Nearby SLAPTON SANDS, BLACKPOOL SANDS and COMPASS COVE provide the beach enthusiast with plenty of scope, while the quay and harbour wall give directly on to the DART ESTUARY. This estuary is something of a fish haven; a worm, crab or fish bait cast well out into the tidal stream will normally catch fish fairly quickly.

Flounders are very common in the Dart, as too are bass and thornback skate. The thornback skate are particularly interesting. They are fairly plentiful, grow to a reasonable size and provide good sport on beach-casting tackle. I find peeler crab is the best bait for these fish, although mackerel fillets can also be effective.

Boat fishing within the Dart estuary can be very productive; bass are often encountered in fair numbers and a light leger baited with sand-eel or ragworm is the best way of catching these fine fish.

Salcombe

To me Salcombe always conjures up memories of magnificent bass catches. Even nowadays, when bass are scarcer than they used to be, Salcombe is still a good bass-fishing

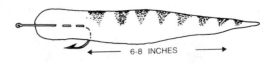

Fig. 8 Mackerel strip cut to resemble a sand-eel.

station. The various beaches provide ample opportunity for shore casting, with ragworm as the best local bait. Apart from bass, Salcombe and its surrounding coastline fishes well for wrasse, conger, skate, flatfish, mackerel and pollack. Inshore-boat fishing can be good. Live sand-eels make the best bait but at a pinch elongated slivers of mackerel cut to resemble a sand-eel (see fig. 8) will catch plenty of good fish.

Boat fishermen at Salcombe often catch a bonus fish in the shape of a huge turbot. The grounds off Salcombe are in fact ideally suited for turbot and many of these succulent flatfish fall to baits intended for bass.

At DOWNDERRY there is plenty of scope for all styles of rock fishing and I have had some good pollack in this area on artificial lures.

Plymouth to Mevagissey

During the past decade, West Country ports such as Plymouth, Looe, Fowey and Mevagissey have become the Mecca of boat anglers from all over the British Isles and the Continent. Charter-boat skippers on this rich and varied coastline have discovered and developed a veritable angling gold mine by finding and fishing the many and varied wrecks of two world wars, and various natural maritime disasters.

The coasts of Devon and Cornwall have always been rich in wrecks, but it is the rusting hulks of comparatively modern vessels that now provide fishing of unbelievable quality. Catches in excess of 2,000 lb or even 3,000 lb of big fish are common when wreck fishing and sport of this quality has acted like a magnet to bring in anglers from all walks of life to fish over untapped wreck marks which could easily produce record catches or record individual fish.

Most of these wrecks are situated far out in the Channel and visiting anglers have come to automatically assume that it is essential to steam four to six hours out before good catches can be expected. This is far from the truth. The wreck marks may well produce big fish in unbelievable numbers but that does not mean that shore anglers and inshore boat fishermen do not also get their share of good fish and bumper catches. To the wreck-fishing fraternity conger, ling and pollack are the predominant species. The inshore angler has a much wider range of fish available and he is not tied by weather and tidal conditions. The result is that although local shore and inshore catches are normally completely overshadowed by the crammed fish holds of the wreck-fishing boats, the inshore fisherman goes quietly about his business catching plenty of very good fish from neglected shore and boat marks.

For the shore- and inshore-boat angler, the most common fish are wrasse, conger, bass, pollack, mullet, ray, mackerel, garfish and a host of lesser fish, all of which provide good catches for those anglers who are prepared to fish hard for them.

Plymouth

Shore-fishing marks to head for in this area are BOLT TAIL to the east of Plymouth, STOKE POINT and RAME HEAD, on the mouth of the Yealm. The beautiful Yealm estuary is a good area to dig worm bait and the river mouth itself is a fine place to fish.

Like most estuaries, the Yealm produces a good selection of fish species. Plaice and, during the winter, heavyweight flounders are often caught in fair quantities and for the angler with bigger fish in mind, running leger tackle baited with fish strip or sand-eel bait will attract good-sized thornback skate and some really hefty specimen small-eyed ray. These small-eyed rays are well worth concentrating on, for, as they are a comparatively rare species, any fish of over about 12 lb could easily earn its captor a prize rod or reel either from the angling papers or the Sunday newspapers. On top of this, there is always the chance of breaking the existing rod-caught record for the species, for very big small-eyed ray are known to use the Yealm area as a feeding ground.

Unlike thornback ray, which tend to be out-and-out scavengers, the small-eyed ray is a comparatively fussy eater. The best bait for this species is a really fresh, large sand-eel. Anglers who take the trouble to catch or obtain sand-eel bait stand a far greater chance of success than those who are content to use strips of stale mackerel as bait. This is understandable, for the ray expect to find sand-eel shoals in the river mouth and to a certain extent they become pre-occupied with this one form of food.

Rame Head

This headland, one of the biggest natural projections in the English Channel, provides an excellent base for all kinds of rock-fishing expeditions. Big wrasse are common off the Rame and good pollack, bass and conger can also be caught. Many anglers may be surprised at the idea that large congers can be caught from the shore, but at many points on this coastline the rocks drop sheer away into very deep water. Many rock gullies hold a fair depth of water even at low tide, and will produce surprisingly large conger. Conger eels are by nature a rock-living species and the tumbled granite rocks off the Devon and particularly Cornish coastline provide them with ample shelter and a super-abundant food supply in the shape of wrasse, pollack, crabs and worms.

Rock fishing for conger is a rough, tough occupation that calls for heavy tackle and a lot of brute force. A well-hooked conger putting up a frantic, last-ditch fight for its life is no respecter of light tackle or the rules of angling. If you decide on a bout of West Country conger fishing from the shore, then make absolutely certain that your tackle has enough backbone to force the eels out of their natural stronghold. I use a 12-ft beach-caster capable of throwing 8- to 10-oz leads. This rod, strong as it may seem when seen in action, has still failed on one or two occasions to prise bigger-than-average conger out of awkward gullies. I use 35-lb line as standard when rock-casting for conger and have a natural preference for braided line rather than monofilament. Long casting as such is seldom necessary, so I do not find the braided line a handicap in this respect. On top of this, the braided line is virtually stretch-free and slightly more buoyant than plain monofilament, both of which, in my opinion, are extremely good virtues. The lack of line stretch is vital when congering in confined conditions.

Even in a large rock gully any conger which picks up a hook bait can only be a yard or two away from a safe retreat. A line which stretches as much as most brands of plain monofilament gives a hooked eel every chance of gaining a safe sanctuary and once this occurs the angler has little choice except to pull for a break. With a non-stretch braided line this is less likely to occur, for, provided you do not hook a monster eel, the fish can be pulled out into open water the moment the strike is made. Being slightly more buoyant than monofilament, braided line has a tendency to sink rather more slowly and come to rest gently on top of weed and rough rock rather than settling heavily into any obstruction it comes into contact with. This buoyancy allows the angler to feel bites more easily and I find that, on the retrieve, it helps to keep the line clear of the rocks.

Having experimented at great length in this respect, I discovered that there were fewer serious 'hang-ups' per session when using the braided line than when using plain nylon monofilament. Braided line is more expensive than nylon, although I feel it is worth the extra cost. Big baits on size 6-0 or even 8-0 hooks to 12 in. wire traces are essential for conger fishing. I use a swivel to join the trace to the line and let this swivel act as a stop for the sliding lead. Long traces have no place in rock gully conger fishing and the 12 in. between hook and sliding lead is ample for this style of fishing.

Looe

Traditional home of the Cornish shark fleet and the Shark Club, Looe has plenty to offer the angler. For those who like to ring the changes as much as possible, Looe is an ideal base. Float fishing from the BANJO PIER will produce mackerel, pollack and wrasse, while in the river mouth it is possible to bottom fish for flounders and the odd plaice.

To add spice to a holiday, it is not a bad idea to have a day out on a Looe sharking boat, or book a seat on a charter boat that specialises in reef fishing. Weather provided, many of these reef-fishing boats operate over marks situated near the EDDYSTONE LIGHTHOUSE. This is a most exciting area to fish. Anglers who own their own boats and have a reasonable amount of sea experience might well like to try their hand at bass fishing off the Eddystone Reef. The Reef has recently produced a new record bass and local anglers regularly return to port with bumper catches of huge bass. The local technique is to slowly troll a rubber eel on a leadless line, training the eel 60 to 80 yards behind a slowly-moving boat. Bass caught in this way have every opportunity to show off their fighting ability to the full, and a big fish can provide a lot of anxious moments before it is anywhere near ready for netting.

Red-gill sand-eels and Eddystone (rubber) eels are favourite lures but at a pinch anything which has a good lively action should catch fish. Strangely enough, although boats from Looe, Plymouth and Mevagissey regularly make the trip out to the Eddystone in search of bass, only a handful of local specialists fish for this species from or close to the shore.

Fowey

This port is the only exception. It has long since been noted for its bass fishing and it is usually possible to hire a self-drive boat to take full advantage of the bass marks within the river itself as well as out in the open sea. Fowey bass specialists normally use live sand-eels as bait, although for the reef marks outside the river, artificial eels have proved to be highly effective. The estuary of the Fowey offers immense possibility for all sorts of fishing, although bass are the most sought-after species.

Most local fishermen net their sand-eel supplies up at GOLANT and if you do not have access to a sand-eel net it is usually easy enough to obtain a quantity of live eels from a local source. Obtaining good-quality eels is easy; keeping them alive and in good condition is a different matter entirely. The habitual bass fishermen of the area make and use a special wooden container known as a *courge* for their sand-eel supplies. This wooden bait-box is kept floating in the water and at all times is towed behind the boat on the way from one mark to the next. Sand-eels are ultra-sensitive creatures and will die rapidly at the slightest lack of oxygen or flow of clean water through the container. They are also very susceptible to disease. For this reason, anglers building their own sand-eel *courge* are advised to burn holes through the sides and top of the box with a heated rod rather than bore them out. The burning process effectively seals the wood and to a certain extent prevents slime and other harmful substances from building up in the inlet holes and killing the eels. For the same reason leather hinges are used instead of metal ones: leather does not rust and the eels do not die from metal poisoning.

61

Almost anywhere between the actual mouth of the Fowey estuary and Golant is likely to produce good bass fishing and a favourite local trick is to motor up to Golant on a rising tide, then drift gently back down on the ebb tide. The sand-eels are fished on 10- or 15-ft nylon traces held down by small, bomb-shaped leads. When bass fishing in this way from a drifting boat it is seldom necessary to use weights larger than an ounce, and it is often possible to fish with far less weight. For this style of fishing, a 9-ft or 10-ft spinning rod and a centre-pin reel loaded with 8- to 10-lb b.s. line makes an ideal and extremely sporting combination. Fowey river bass regularly weigh in at upwards of 6 lb and a fish of this size hooked on the tackle described will put up a staggering show of strength and sheer fighting ability before it can be subdued enough for netting.

Outside the harbour entrance to the east lies the UDDER REEF. This rough ground is a small-boat bass fisherman's paradise, for bass of all sizes congregate in huge shoals over and round the reef area and it is from the Udder that some of the truly huge bags of big bass are made. On many occasions, Fowey bass men have returned from the Udder Reef with more than sixty big bass to show for a day's angling. Fortunately, this mass slaughter is now quickly becoming less fashionable as anglers become more conservation-minded. I have fished on the Udder Reef when the bass packs have gone absolutely wild and the fish were so suicidal that I am absolutely certain they would have snatched at totally bare hooks.

Apart from its magnificent bass fishing, Fowey River holds a wide variety of sport fish. Conger, some being of prodigious size, lurk round the quays, jetties and river marks and the river is often thick with good-sized thornback skate. Small-boat anglers often tie up to the huge buoys below the china-clay jetties and it is from these mid-river marks that the main skate catches are made. To catch skate consistently in the Fowey the best bait to use is soft-back or peeler crab. These moulting crabs can be collected at low water from under weed-covered rocks. The foreshore below the jetty at Golant is an ideal crab-collecting area, although at a pinch almost any likely section of foreshore will do.

Fowey anglers use an interesting technique when baiting up with crab. Instead of pushing the hook through the soft shell and body of the crab they run the hook point and bend

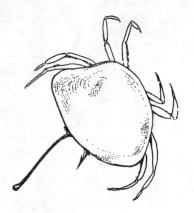

Fig. 9   Crab hooked behind eye sockets.

through behind the eye sockets of the bait (see fig. 9). This provides a good hook hold without breaking up the bait.

For the angler who prefers a more active style of fishing, flounder and plaice provide the ideal targets. These interesting, active flatfish can be caught either from the shore or from a boat. The most killing technique for both fish is to spin with a very large baited-spoon rig. The stretch of the river known as SAWMILLS is the best place for big 'flatties' and it is from this point, approximately midway between Golant and Fowey, that many immense specimen flounders have been taken.

Local anglers use an interestingly enlarged version of the conventional flatfish spoon rig to take these extra-large

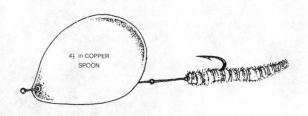

4½ in COPPER
SPOON

Fig. 10   Plaice spoon baited with worm.

flounders. This consists of a $4\frac{1}{2}$ in. home-made copper spoon which replaces the normal metal or white plastic spoon or the shop-bought baited spoon. This huge copper spinner with its trailing worm (see fig. 10) has proved to be an absolute winner on the Fowey River and anyone who is handy with tools can easily knock up a few of these big spoons from oddments of copper sheet.

The grey mullet is very common in the Fowey River, vast shoals being present throughout the summer and early autumn months. Few anglers try to catch these elusive fish, for Fowey mullet—like all grey mullet—have a reputation for being uncatchable. Mullet are unquestionably difficult to catch, but they can be taken, and in quantity, provided the angler is prepared to think hard about his fishing and then put in long, hard hours in an attempt to induce the mullet shoals to feed. I can remember spending hours watching the shoaling mullet from the railway track that runs beside the Fowey River at Golant. The fish were obviously feeding, for they followed the advancing tides in across the rapidly covering mudflats, pushing along in water too shallow to cover their backs. Time and again it was possible to see the fish opening their strange mouths as they sucked in particles of food.

I was convinced in my own mind that fish which behaved in this fashion could be caught provided they were first induced to accept some substitute for their normal food. Mullet are soft-mouthed fish that like soft-textured baits. They suck rather than bite at food and for this reason they have a natural inclination towards soft, easily-swallowed edible matter. Bread has always attracted mullet and these Fowey fish were no exception. Initially, I attracted and held their attention by anchoring breadcrusts in their normal feeding areas. To begin with the fish shied away from the bread, then their curiosity got the better of them and soon each anchored crust was surrounded by a jostling, splashing horde of avidly feeding fish. Having induced the fish to accept bread, my next step was to catch them. Obviously the mullet were surface feeding, so float fishing seemed the best way of presenting the bait. From my vantage point on the railway embankment I could clearly see the mullet shoals swimming beneath the anchored breadcrust. Many of the fish were feeding on crumbs of bread that were breaking off the crust, so in an attempt to present the bait

BUDE

NEWQUAY

MEVAGISSEY

PENZANCE

FALMOUTH

LANDS
END

LIZARD
POINT

as naturally as possible I fished with a river-sized, self-cocking float. Mullet shy away from thick lines, so I used a roach rod, 3-lb b.s. line and fixed-spool reel—basic, average freshwater gear.

Baiting up with a tiny pinch of soft bread, I set the float 12 in. above the hook and cast out so that float and bait dropped into the water directly alongside the anchored bread-crust. The totally weightless line below the float allowed the bread bait to fall naturally through the water, and as the float began to sit up, a fish sucked in the bait, causing the float to glide gently out of sight. Bites like this are normally difficult to miss, but mullet are adept at sucking off baits without getting hooked in the process and this fish was no exception. Cursing my luck at missing the first good bite of the day, I wound in, re-baited the tiny hook and cast back out to the shoaling fish. This time I actually saw a mullet take the bait and as the bread bait vanished I struck hard and set the hook firmly into a good fish.

Mullet are tremendously powerful fighters and the moment my fish felt the hook in its mouth it rocketed off down-river, making my reel clutch scream like a banshee. A big mullet hooked in shallow water is a real handful and

C

this first fish of the day really showed its speed and endurance, making run after desperate run in its attempt to shake free of the restraining hook. When I first hooked the fish, the disturbance had caused the main shoal to scatter in alarm. Now they had re-grouped under the bread, obviously feeding seriously. Having taken my time with this first fish, I wore it down slowly so that by the time it was ready for the landing net it was too exhausted to put up any sort of last-ditch struggle. With fish number one in the bag, I was soon back in action, finishing up with a total of six fish landed, two fish lost by breakages and a dozen or so totally missed bites. By mullet fishing standards, the session was a winner and any angler in the Fowey area who is interested in a bout of light-tackle fishing will be well advised to take a long, hard look at the mullet shoals that frequent the river.

Since my initial success I have gone on to take big mullet from POLRUAN and several jetties along the river. Obviously the whole of the river is alive with big, hard-fighting mullet, for fish of nearly 7 lb have been caught on occasion and much larger fish have been hooked and lost.

Par

Situated between Fowey and St Austell, PAR offers plenty of beach fishing for plaice, bass and the occasional sole. Bass fishing can be very good at times, particularly after a gale when the water has been churned up to a soup-like consistency. Similar in many ways is the beach at PENTEWAN nearer to Mevagissey. I have had excellent catches of smallish bass from this beach and during the early part of the year some good-sized plaice in the bay make a welcome addition to the day's fishing. Ragworm can be dug at Pentewan and local anglers often dig over the beach to get white ragworm, an absolutely deadly fish catcher.

Mevagissey

Long famous as a holiday and fishing centre, MEVAGISSEY is nowadays one of the main wreck-fishing and shark-fishing ports in the West Country and big boats leave the port daily, bound for distant water wrecks.

Not all the fishing round Mevagissey has to be done from big boats—the whole of the bay area offers ample opportunity for small-boat fishermen to try their luck. I have had good catches of pollack, conger, mackerel, garfish, dogfish and wrasse while fishing at various points round the bay. The rocks adjacent to the headland at CHAPEL POINT are often thick with fair-sized pollack which can be caught on feathers or on ragworm. Worm bait used in this area invariably produces some big wrasse to add interest to the day's fishing. Self-drive boats can be hired in the outer harbour, which is useful if you only want an hour or two's fishing.

For the shore-fishing enthusiast, Mevagissey and its adjacent beaches can provide tremendous fishing. To the east, and only reachable by a long walk up past the coastguard station, lie two very isolated beaches, BIG POLSTREATH and LITTLE POLSTREATH. These are divided by a spear-point of rock which in turn is split. The outer end of this natural barrier is a good place to fish on a falling tide but care must be taken to move back as the tide begins to rise, otherwise it is possible to get cut off completely from the shore. Polstreath can on occasion produce a wide variety of fish. Bass, including some very big fish, often frequent this beach and on the rocky extremities of either beach wrasse and pollack can usually be caught in quantity.

On one occasion, I was wrasse fishing in the numerous rock gullies at the eastern end of Big Polstreath Beach when I noticed what looked like a huge sheet of brown paper resting amongst the thick kelp beds on a gully bottom. Seconds later the 'brown paper' rose to the surface and turned into a really huge angler fish. At a rough estimate I would have put the weight of this monster at 70 lb or more. Armed only with standard wrasse fishing gear, I knew I had little chance of holding such a fish, but I was determined to try. Hook it I did and for a moment or two I felt I had a chance of working it round to shallow water and then beaching it. Unfortunately the fish, realising its danger, abruptly turned and surged off out to sea. Ten-pound b.s. line is hardly the sort of gear to use on a big angler fish and the last I saw or felt of this monster was a thrashing of white water and a savage jerk which broke my line like so much rotten cotton.

Mevagissey Harbour area is well worth looking at. The

LIGHTHOUSE QUAY and the ISLAND QUAY on the east side of the harbour entrance provide plenty of scope for the shore fisherman. Float fishing for mackerel and garfish is a favourite style of angling from the Lighthouse Quay, strips of fresh mackerel and garfish making the best bait. Similar tactics using worm baits on either the Lighthouse Quay or the Island Quay produce wrasse in plenty and the occasional pollack and big bass. Both quays have produced bass and pollack of over 10 lb, often caught by anglers who have been fishing for mackerel.

The two quays at Mevagissey provide good bottom fishing, particularly for conger eels. In years gone by the Lighthouse Quay has produced conger of over 70 lb on heavy hand-line tackle, and rod and line anglers have taken conger to 50 lb from this same quay. Catches of four or more good eels in a single evening's fishing are commonplace for marks outside, and inside the harbour walls are alive with congers in the 10-lb to 25-lb range. Much heavier eels are present but more often than not these monsters manage to break free when hooked.

I actually lost what I consider to be the largest conger I have ever hooked while fishing over the seaward side of the Lighthouse Jetty. This fish which I hooked after midnight on a warm, thundery night fought a solid running battle for just under forty-five minutes. Twice I managed to steer it round inside the harbour in the vain hope that one of my companions would be able to go down the stone steps to water level and gaff the fish. On each occasion the conger turned before it could be brought within gaffing range and ran back into open water again. On the third try, I was sure the fish was just about finished, then it turned yet again and began to make a long impressively slow run back out to sea. Try as I might, I could not stop the fish until finally in sheer desperation I clamped hard down in an attempt to stop the mighty eel from going to ground in the foundations of what had once been the original quay wall. The result was that my heavy rod snapped clean in two and the tip section vanished down the line at high speed. Left only with the shattered stump of my rod, I just could not stop the eel from reaching its objective and finally I had to resort to hand lining until the heavy braided line parted.

How big that conger was I shall never know, but I did have a 45-lb eel from the same place on lighter tackle which was played out, gaffed and on top of the quay in just fifteen minutes. Apart from totally ruining a good rod, the big conger also buckled the reel seating so badly that the reel was a total write-off. Whether or not monster conger still lurk round the Mevagissey quays I do not know, but I do know that there are still plenty of biggish eels to be caught round the walls for any angler who is prepared to fish after dark for them.

Apart from the fish already mentioned, many other species of fish can occasionally be caught round the quay walls. I have had red bream, dogfish, john-dory, horse mackerel, mullet, plaice, big wrasse and many smaller species as well. The Lighthouse Quay, facing the open sea, can also spring the occasional surprise. One lucky angler fishing a light, single-hook nylon paternoster rig struck at a gentle bite and found himself firmly attached to a monster turbot. This fish surprisingly enough was played out and gaffed on extremely light line. Later it officially tipped the scales at a fraction over 18 lb. Yet another angler, bottom fishing for conger, hooked a heavy slow-moving fish which subsequently turned out to be a 43-lb monkfish.

Over the hill from Mevagissey, the tiny beach at PORT-MELLON COVE can provide some fair fishing for small bass and the occasional conger. This beach is a good place to rake for live sand-eels. Port Mellon is also useful as a place to leave a car before starting the long walk out to the magnificent rock gullies round CHAPEL POINT. This is a favourite headland with wrasse anglers for the many, often easily accessible rock gullies around Chapel Point can, if fished properly, produce immense catches of big wrasse. The best ways to wrasse-fish this area are to float fish or paternoster a hard-backed crab bait in the deeper gullies. Anglers who prefer to catch other fish will find spinning for pollack and the occasional bass most rewarding.

I was once sent a box of beautifully-made American plug baits which I decided to try from the rocks round Chapel Point. Having never before used this kind of bait in salt water, I was interested to find out whether or not they would work. I started with a huge, three-jointed plug but did not have a strike. I then switched to a blue-and-white double-jointed effort that wiggled seductively through the water at the slightest pull from the rod top. Second cast with this lure produced interest—a trio of good-sized bass trailing along directly astern of the bait. Unfortunately they sheered away when they saw me above them. Next cast I punched the bait out farther and began to retrieve line in short, sharp bursts. Thirty yards from the rocks the line went suddenly tight and I thought I had snagged bottom, then a vicious yank at the rod top warned me I was into a fish and ten minutes later in came a magnificent 6-lb bass, mouth agape, plug bait dangling, the hooks firmly embedded in its hard mouth. This is living proof that spining or plug-bait fishing off Chapel Point is well worth trying.

Between Chapel Point and the massive loom of the DODMAN POINT lies a wealth of good fishing. Rock-fishing enthusiasts are well advised to explore the entire area, for pollack, wrasse, bass and conger are common in all the deeper gullies and light-float fishing from ledges which face directly out to sea will produce mackerel and big garfish as well.

Whenever I visit this area I take two sets of tackle, one lightweight outfit which I use for the smaller species and a beach-caster which I bait up with mackerel fillet and cast out into the deeper gullies. Basically this heavy outfit is intended for conger, but the big hook, baited with mackerel fillet, will also produce bass—not the usual run of 1-lb to 3-lb fish, but thumping great 6- to 9-pounders which run off yard after yard of line before I even have time to pick up the rod. Naturally, these big bass are far from common but there are enough of them to make big-bait fishing a really worthwhile occupation. Several small beaches along this stretch of rich and varied coastline are also worth trying for bass, particularly after dark. Standard leger tackle is the ideal terminal rig to use. Hook size depends, of course, on the kind of bait being employed. With big fillet baits I use 6–0 hooks, whereas with worm bait a size 2–0 or 3–0 is best. If you can find a deep rock gully that has a sandy bottom, legering with worm bait could easily produce some big plaice. Most of this coastline to too rocky for commercial boats to trawl and isolated pockets of big flatfish do occur.

Off GORRAN HAVEN there is plenty to interest the small-boat angler. The varied nature of the sea bed in this area provides a rich feeding ground for many kinds of fish. Off-shore, the stark GWINEAS ROCK is worth trying on calm days for bass and big pollack. Bottom fishing throughout the bay will produce dogfish, skate, conger, bull huss, wrasse, tope, pollack and red bream. Spinning or trolling is often used here to take big bass, mackerel, garfish and pollack. The bass and pollack normally fall to red-gill eels trolled well behind the boat.

Mevagissey, Falmouth, Newquay and Bude

Between Mevagissey and Falmouth miles of craggy indented coastline provides a wealth of almost untapped fishing: beaches, bays, coves and rock gullies proliferate in a wild confusion of rugged scenery that makes the south coast of Cornwall such a fantastically scenic back-drop for angling activities. This is wrasse, bass and big conger country *par excellence*. Almost any part of this coastline fishes well and, as I have already stated, much of its potential is at best barely scratched by local and visiting fishermen.

This is a coastline which can produce surprise catches. More than one monster angler fish has been taken by shore fishermen here and at times, particularly in the late autumn, some very hefty conger move inshore to feed within casting range of the rocks. Much of this coastline is controlled by the National Trust and most of the sea-shore is accessible by public footpaths. However, many good fishing spots are quite a hike from the nearest car park and many involve awkward scrambles down fairly steep cliffs. Because of these natural hazards, much of the fishing is unexploited. Anglers who do not mind a walk and a scramble will discover many hot-spot sites that rarely get fished more than once a season. For the less adventurous there are innumerable bays and rocky areas within easy range of car-parking facilities. During the summer months most beaches are crowded, but as Cornish beaches tend to be flanked by rock outcrops it is often possible to scramble over the rocks to fish comparatively deep water out beyond the bathing areas.

Falmouth

Basically a boat-fishing centre, Falmouth and its adjacent harbour area offers little for the shore fisherman, the only exception being mullet. Mullet can be taken in PENRYN

71

HARBOUR, or from the Customs House Quay or the Prince of Wales Pier. Boat fishing inside Falmouth harbour can be quite good, flatfish, bass and the occasional skate being the most common species encountered.

Penzance

Unlike Falmouth, Penzance has a great deal to offer the shore fisherman. For miles on either side of the town there are plenty of good shore-fishing venues. Penzance is an ideal point from which to reach both the south and north coast fishing grounds. TREEN, SENNEN COVE, LOGAN ROCKS, EASTERN GREEN, ST MICHAEL'S MOUNT, PORTH CURNA and LOOE BAR are just a very few of the many productive fishing spots that are situated within striking range. Most of these spots are easily reachable, but there are dozens of less accessible places, all of which can provide good fishing with either beach-casting, float fishing or spinning tackle.

Cornwall is the ideal place for the freshwater angler to try his luck with sea angling. In most places it is more than possible to fish with pike or leger-type rods and matching reels. Even the dedicated light-tackle angler who normally match-fishes on some northern canal can bring his delicate match tackle and refined techniques to Cornwall and fish for mullet. Many anglers who have done this have since become dedicated sea anglers. Bait can be dug on most of the beaches in the Penzance area. Lugworm is the favourite local bait. Sand-eels can be raked at Sennen Cove.

Newquay

Rapidly making a name for itself as a shark-fishing centre, Newquay and its adjacent area has a great deal to offer the visiting angler. The north coast of Cornwall is good for bass fishing and Newquay's adjacent beaches provide ample scope for shore casting.

The beaches to head for are GREAT WESTERN, FISTRAL, WATERGATE, TOWAN, TOLCARNE, PORTH, LUSTY GLAZE, CRANTOCK and WHIPSIDERRY. Apart from these spots there is plenty of rock fishing available, but be careful: big seas are common and to avoid serious accidents due to high tides or freak wave patterns, the rock angler should only fish in calm weather and even the he must keep an eye on tide flow and wave action.

Most local anglers travel to TREVOSE HEAD for serious rock fishing. Trevose Head is noted for wrasse, tope and small-eyed ray. The tope and small-eyed ray are normally caught on leger tackle baited with fresh sand-eel. The big wrasse fall mainly to worm or crab bait. Tope fishing the Trevose Head area is most exciting. Local specialists use ultra-light tackle to take heavyweight specimens and a big tope hooked on 15-lb b.s. line is capable of putting up a tremendous struggle when hooked. A single sand-eel may sound a small bait to offer a big fish like a tope, but this shark frequents the area simply to take advantage of the sand-eel shoals that infest this section of coastline. Because of this preoccupation with sand-eels as a staple food-supply, tope irrespective of size will take a natural eel in preference to bigger, more conventional baits, such as whole or filleted mackerel. Trevose Head can easily produce tope and small-eyed ray in excess of the present record sizes.

The north and south quays of Newquay Harbour are worth fishing, particularly for mackerel, bass, garfish, mullet, conger and wrasse. Small-boat fishing is not to be recommended anywhere round the Newquay or for that matter anywhere along the north Cornish coastline which faces directly out into the Atlantic. Bad tides and heavy seas are extremely common and unless you are a very experienced boat handler with intimate knowledge of this rugged coastline it is very easy to get into serious and possibly fatal trouble very quickly indeed.

Bude

Bude is another good fishing centre. Beaches like WIDE-MOUTH BAY, SUMMERLEAZE BEACH, SANDY MOUTH and CROOK-LETS BEACH are all good for bass and flatfish catching. The breakwater at Summerleaze is worth a try, although it seldom fishes as well as the beaches.

Boat fishing off Bude is often difficult, although by picking the right conditions and keeping a weather eye open it is possible to go afloat. Boat fishermen anchoring or drifting over local inshore marks take mackerel, garfish, pollack,

73

bass, flatfish, conger eels, tope, wrasse and pouting. Best baits are again live or freshly killed sand-eels. If these are unobtainable, strips or fillets of mackerel make a good substitute. For shore fishing, ragworm, lugworm and peeler crab make the best baits.

Bristol Channel and South Wales

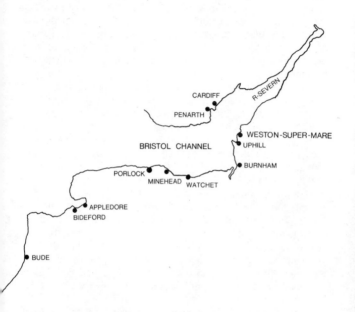

Bude to Cardiff

North of Bude the coastline becomes increasingly rugged, providing ample scope for a wide variety of fishing possibilities. Local boats operating along this coastline take immense catches of large porbeagle shark, fish weighing over 200 lb being relatively common.

Bideford and Appledore

Both these ports now provide charter-boat services which concentrate mainly on porbeagle shark fishing. At times these sharks are so numerous over the inshore grounds that they make a considerable and dangerous nuisance of themselves to dinghy and small-boat anglers. A favourite trick of the local shark population is to snatch at mackerel or pollack which have been hooked by boat-fishing anglers. The shark are so persistent that at times anglers are forced to stop fishing and go back to port to avoid the fish-stealing porbeagles.

Naturally a big, angry shark hooked from a small boat can be a nasty customer to deal with and few anglers care to match tackle and strength with these giants from the confines of a small boat. I remember one occasion when I was dinghy fishing this area and pollack were coming thick and fast. Every drop down resulted in a well-hooked fish, not monsters but useful 4-lb to 6-lb specimens which put a satisfying bend in my light rod. Suddenly, just as I was winding a reasonable fish to the surface, I felt a tremendous weight come on to the line. There was no savage tug, no rod-breaking snatch, just the impression that something of immense size had fouled up the line. Looking over the side down through the crystal-clear water, I found myself directly above a big shark, and jammed across its gash of a mouth was the still-struggling pollack. I realised I had no chance of holding this vast fish on my light tackle, so I waited while it gulped down my catch.

Seconds after the fish disapeared into its mouth, my light line parted, obviously severed by the shark's razor-sharp teeth. To give the fish time to vacate the area, I took my time in re-tackling. Finally satisfied that it had gone, I re-baited, dropped my tackle down to the bottom and almost immediately hooked another pollack. Pumping the fish to the surface, I was just about to gaff it into the boat when the water erupted as a large shark literally snatched the fish from under my nose. I thought that in all probability this was the same shark that had robbed me of my earlier catch, but looking into the water I could see at least four heavy-weight porbeagles cruising about directly beneath the boat. The sharks were obviously well on the feed, and knowing full well that they would take every fish I hooked, I realised that further sport was out of the question, so I packed up and came on inshore.

Big, hungry sharks can quickly become a dangerous proposition; it is not that they might attack the boat, but in their effort to snatch at hooked fish they might easily damage or even upset a small boat and I did not relish the thought of being tipped into the water.

Quite apart from shark, the Bideford–Appledore area is basically a good fishing locality. There is good shore fishing, particularly for bass and flatfish. Favourite local stations are GREYSAND, the estuary of the River Torridge near the iron railway bridge. For the pier-harbour angler BIDEFORD QUAY is well worth a visit. Apart from the fish already mentioned, the offshore grounds yield skate, tope, conger, ling, black and red bream, dogfish, flatfish, pouting and the occasional cod.

Minehead

Facing directly out into the Bristol Channel, Minehead should fish better than it does, but ultra-fast tides and fairly shallow water makes this section of coastline rather bad for anglers. On occasions, good-sized conger, bass and flatfish are caught from Minehead Harbour Wall, DUNSTER BEACH, MADBRAIN BEACH or the horribly-named GASWORKS BEACH. From time to time immense conger eels are washed up along this coastline. In all probability these dead or dying giants come drifting inshore from one of the many wrecks which litter the Bristol Channel. Some of these eels weigh up to 100 lb.

Small-boat fishing off Minehead is very difficult. Raging tides make it unsafe in anything other than perfect conditions. Charter boats fishing offshore grounds take good catches of prime thornback skate, bull huss, cod, tope, conger and sea bream. The best tackle for boat fishing is a single hooking running leger baited with fish or squid. For shore fishing worm or crab baits should be employed.

Watchet

Similar in many ways to Minehead, Watchet and its adjacent coastline is seldom very productive. Tides are exceptionally fierce and amateur boatmen are advised to take great care at all times. Shore fishing at BLUE ANCHOR BEACH and ST AUDRIE'S BAY can produce flatfish and small bass. It is generally a very uninteresting area to fish. Good-sized lugworm can be dug at Blue Anchor Bay and isolated pockets of big ragworm can be found off Watchet Harbour.

Bridgwater and Weston Super Mare

There is comparatively good shore fishing all the way along this section of coastline. BURNHAM-ON-SEA town beach, HINKLEY REEF, RIVER PARRET ESTUARY, BREAN DOWN, the toll road from WESTON to SAND BAY are all worth a try. This is mainly bass, flatfish and silver eel territory and the best baits to use are ragworm or lugworm. At times the silver-eel fishing can be very good, particularly during the late summer and early autumn period. Silver eels, which are really migrating river eels, tend to bite freely provided the bait is anchored hard on the bottom.

To avoid difficult tangles, my advice is to use a single-hook leger rig. Multi-hook terminal rigs give the incredibly slippery eels every opportunity to twist and tangle the line into an obnoxious ball of slime-covered nylon. For the pier anglers, the old pier at WESTON, KNIGHTSTONE HARBOUR and the STOLFORD TO HINKLEY SEA WALL make good stations. Small-boat fishing is fairly good, mackerel, skate, flatfish, cod, conger and tope being caught. BRISTOL itself is hardly worth considering from the fishing point of view.

Boat fishing in the BRISTOL CHANNEL is seldom very good, although good fish do occasionally occur. Strong tides and coloured water make fishing difficult at the best of times and my advice to boat anglers is to look elsewhere for your sport.

Cardiff, Swansea, Milford Haven and Fishguard

The fishing in the Cardiff area can hardly be described as good. Even so, it is possible to catch flounder, plaice, dabs and the occasional sole and cod in the vicinity. The Cardiff foreshore and Cardiff Docks can only be fished by permit

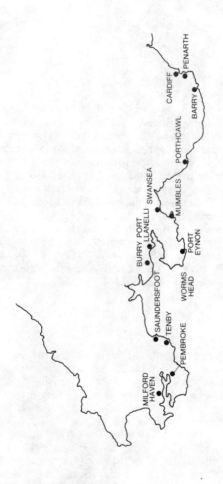

CARDIFF
PENARTH
BARRY
PORTHCAWL
SWANSEA
LLANELLI
MUMBLES
BURRY PORT
PORT EYNON
WORMS HEAD
SAUNDERSFOOT
TENBY
PEMBROKE
MILFORD HAVEN

holders who must pay a nominal annual figure for this dubious privilege. Permits are obtainable from the Dock Manager's office and at the time of writing they cost £1.00.

Although sea fishing around Cardiff is far from good, the fishing improves rapidly as you move farther along round the coastline.

Penarth

Similar in many ways to Cardiff as far as fishing potential is concerned, Penarth has one or two beaches that occasionally fish quite well. LAVERNOCK BEACH is generally quite reliable and the pebble beaches adjacent to Penarth fish well during the winter months for smallish cod and fair-sized whiting. Penarth Pier is hardly a hot-spot fishing platform but it does occasionaly produce good results, again mostly during the winter-time. This pier is closed to anglers during the peak holiday months of July and August and night fishing is not allowed at any time. One- or two-hook paternoster tackle baited with worm, squid or fish strips is the favourite terminal tackle of local anglers. Favourite local bait is lugworm which can be dug along the foreshore. Boat fishing is something of an unknown quantity.

Barry

From Barry onwards, fishing really begins to improve. Many anglers fish Barry Docks for flounders, whiting, silver eels and the occasional bass. More still use the local beaches and rock-fishing stations. FRIARS POINT, NELL'S POINT, BENDRICK ROCK and COLD KNAP beach are extensively used by anglers. SULLY ISLAND, which can only be reached by a causeway, is another favourite venue. The causeway crossing is dangerous and my advice to newcomers to this area is to fish Sully Island in company with knowledgeable local anglers. Bait worms can be dug from local beaches and from the dock area.

Small boats fishing inshore marks often take fair catches of cod, whiting and flatfish, and tope are also caught.

80

Porthcawl

Situated approximately halfway between Cardiff and Swansea, Porthcawl is generally a good fishing area. The local pier can produce surprisingly heavy bags of good-sized fish. Thornback ray in particular are often caught from this pier.

Some years ago, while on a fishing holiday in Wales, I decided to fish at Porthcawl. Knowing nothing of the area, I decided to start on the pier—always a good way to meet local anglers and learn from them the best places to fish. Being without bait, I bought a couple of rather smelly mackerel from a wet-fish shop. Deciding on a big-fish-or-nothing style of angling, I made up a running leger, tied on a 5–0 hook, baited with a long strip of mackerel, and cast out. Propping my long rod up against a rail, I settled back to wait for a bite. Fifteen minutes passed, then the long rod top dipped heavily. Picking up the rod, I waited for further developments. For a minute or two nothing hapened, then just as I was beginning to think that the fish had gone, the rod tip slammed down as a fish moved off with the big bait. Striking was a formality, simply a matter of swinging the rod top back to set the hook firmly. The moment I felt the fish I knew I was into a skate of some sort. Sure enough after a short but interesting tussle a fine thornback surfaced, turned over on its back and allowed itself to be dragged in towards the pier stanchions.

At this stage a local appeared with a drop net and my fish was soon up to deck level. About 8 lb was my reckoning and my new-found friend assessed the fish at about the same weight. Thornbacks of this size, he told me, were fairly common off the pier and bigger specimens were also taken occasionally. Excited and interested by my catch, I re-baited, cast out again and settled back to wait and watch for further developments.

During the next hour my new friend told me a great deal about the fishing potential of Porthcawl. He said the area consisted of five bays—CONEY BEACH, SKER POINT, MOR-CAR BAY, TRECO BAY and NEWTON BEACH. All five venues apparently fished well and I subsequently found he was right. Pouting, flatfish, bass, whiting and thornback skate were the most common species and, depending on the season, there was always the chance of encountering a big summer tope or a good-sized winter cod. The pier was a good all-round angling station, with thornback skate being the most-sought-after species.

Moments after receiving this last piece of information, I got my second skate bite of the day. Minutes later the fish was in the drop net being hauled quickly up to pier level. It was almost identical to the first fish, and the pair made a satisfying catch. Obviously my rather stale, smelly offering had paid off. Skate are far from fussy feeders and on many occasions I have found thornbacks to be attracted by ripe-smelling baits.

Boat fishing off Porthcawl is well worth trying. Most of the known marks yield good catches of mixed fish. Apart from the more common fish already mentioned, boat fishermen take conger, tope, black bream, dogfish, the occasional turbot and sometimes a big angler fish as well. Charter boats can be booked on the pier or from the beach.

Swansea

Most sea anglers will have heard of the fishing at Swansea. Over the years a great deal has been written in the popular angling press about Swansea and its surrounding area. Swansea has a great deal to offer the visiting angler, but like most places does not fish as well as it used to do. Even so, it is well worth a visit and as a starting point for the GOWER COAST it cannot be beaten. There are enough shore and boat marks in the Swansea area to provide weeks of fishing without bothering to move on to new pastures.

For the less adventurous, MUMBLES PIER, EAST PIER and the QUEEN'S DOCK BREAKWATER are all places worth trying. Permits to fish these places cost £1.00 per annum and can be obtained from the Docks Board, Adelaide Street, Swansea. By fishing the piers and breakwater it is possible to catch conger, pouting, bass, flatfish, mullet, garfish and mackerel. For the get-away-from-the-crowd enthusiast, the local beaches, or better still the rock marks, provide plenty of opportunity for solitude. Marks to head for are WORMS HEAD, PORTEYNON, RHOSSILI, LLANGENNITH, CASWELL and BURY HOLM.

Small boats can be launched at many points and by trial and experiment it is possible to drop on some good fishing.

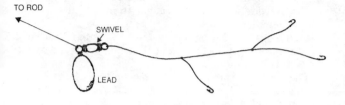

Fig. 11 Treble hook flatfish leger.

Flatfish are still fairly common and by drifting or anchoring and using a light flounder-spoon rig or 1- to 3-hook leger set up (see fig. 11) it is possible to catch some good bags of small to medium-sized flounder, plaice, dabs and even the odd sole. Small-boat fishermen interested in big fish will do well to fish big fish baits in an attempt to get to grips with tope and skate. This whole area is good for both species and by fishing hard with the right bait it is possible to come up with tope weighing over 40 lb.

Various rock marks are good for wrasse fishing, although generally the wrasse in the Gower area tend to be rather on the small side.

Carmarthen Bay

The Carmarthen coastline is truly rich in fishing. Amply endowed with beaches, rocky headlands and similar fishing stations, it is a top-notch venue.

Small-boat fishing can be extremely good in Carmarthen Bay, with tope and thornback ray being the predominant species.

Laugharne

A small town, is adjacent to LAUGHARNE SANDS and PENDINE SANDS, both of which fish well for flatfish, bass and the occasional tope. Farther round the coastline AMROTH BEACH, although smallish, also fishes quite well at times.

SAUNDERSFOOT is noted for its offshore tope grounds, but

83

has plenty to offer in the way of mixed fishing as well. The present record for tope was caught from a boat operating out of Saundersfoot.

Lugworm bait can be dug at LLANELLY BEACH and good ragworm thrive in the estuaries of the TAF, TOWY and GWEN-DREATH RIVERS.

There is reasonable fishing from various quays in the area, and also at BURRY PORT HARBOUR. Bass, mackerel, flat-fish and mullet are the main species caught by harbour anglers.

Tope fishing is extremely good and anglers who are prepared to take the trouble to obtain fresh bait will usually meet with success. Mackerel and flatfish are the favourite local tope baits and, if anything, the flatfish make the best bait, although mackerel are often easier to obtain.

Boats can be launched at Pendine, Ferry Side and Burry Port.

Tenby

Long established as a holiday centre, Tenby has much to attract the keen angler as well. West of Tenby, GILTAR BEACH and Point provide plenty of scope for the bass angler. Another top bass-producing spot is CALDY ISLAND. Caldy can be reached by a ferry service which operates five and a half days a week. These boats leave at thirty-minute intervals, providing a first-class service.

Apart from bass, the area around Tenby fishes well for mackerel, pouting, garfish, flatfish, conger, tope, skate, cod, whiting and wrasse.

For bass fishing, the best bait is soft-back or peeler crab which can be gathered at low tide from the causeway be-tween Caldy Island and ST MARGARET'S ISLAND. Fresh mackerel can usually be purchased from local commercial fishing boats and provided you have time to spare, razor fish can be dug from local beaches.

Milford Haven

Between Tenby and Milford Haven the wild and rugged coastline provides a wealth of rock fishing. STACKPOLE HEAD, ST GOVAN'S HEAD, WINNEY HEAD, FRESHWATER WEST, ANGLE

BAY and the many rock spots in between are barely fished. At one time this used to be top-notch inshore tope country. Nowadays tope are scarcer than they were and most anglers that fish this area concentrate on bass, pollack, wrasse and mackerel, but big tope still visit this area on occasions and anglers who fish a big bait on large hooks stand the chance of making contact with the odd big tope.

Shingle bays at EAST ANGLE, PENNER GUT and MARTIN'S HAVEN are worth trying for skate, tope, bass and flatfish, while in the Milford Haven area there are numerous jetties and rock marks where access can be gained to very deep water. The rocks near the WARRIOR JETTY are worth a try, particularly for bass and conger eels. Strong tides make fishing round the Warrior area rather difficult, but there are some big fish to be found here. Spinning round the Warrior rocks produces fair catches of small to medium-sized bass.

Strong tides make small-boat fishing difficult in the Milford Haven area.

Pembrokeshire Coast

From Milford Haven right up to Fishguard the whole coastline is made up of a magnificent jumble of bays, headlands and deep-water gullies, all of which are well worth fishing. Known only to a few visiting anglers, this beautiful Pembrokeshire coast would take a lifetime to explore thoroughly, but almost any point will provide good fishing. This is essentially a rock-fishing area, although the occasional small beach will be well worth trying for bass. Good thornback ray can also be caught from the beaches in this area. Float fishing from rocks surrounded by deep water will produce pollack, wrasse, mackerel, bass and garfish. Bottom fishing is worth trying for big bass, conger, skate and the occasional tope.

This is essentially a 'get away from it all' coastline, ideal for the camping-fishing holiday of a lifetime.

CHAPTER 5

North Wales and the North West Coast

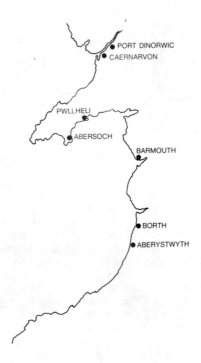

Aberystwyth, Barmouth and the Wirral

Between Fishguard and Cardigan itself lies an interesting and rather beautiful stretch of coastline. DINAS HEAD, and NEWPORT BAY is a good bass-fishing area with the chance of catching other fish as well, DINAS DINGLE, an isolated shingly beach, is a real surf-fishing hot-spot. Best fished at night, this area is capable of producing bass up to and over 10 lb.

Beyond Cardigan, the towns of ABERPORTH, NEW QUAY, ABERAYRON and LLANSANTFFRAID are all situated in good mixed-fishing areas. This whole coast is still something of an unknown quantity. There is very little boat fishing and shore anglers have only just scratched the surface of the general fishing potential. Some of the best beach catches are made at night by visiting anglers and some concentrated effort would undoubtedly show that night fishing could easily produce exceptional results with a wide variety of good big fish.

Aberystwyth

Despite its popularity as a holiday resort, Aberystwyth has much to offer the shore angler. YNYS-LAS BEACH, BORTH BEACH, TAN-Y-BACH BEACH, CONSTITUTION HILL ROCKS and CASTLE ROCKS all provide the shore angler with plenty of oportunity for angling and by careful picking and choosing it is normally possible to get away from the holiday crowds. As an alternative to beach or rock marks, Aberystwyth's stone pier is worth trying, particularly at night. Bass and flatfish are the most common species in the area and a light one or two-hook leger rig baited with peeler crab, lugworm, or cockles will usually produce results. Worms and cockles can be dug from Borth Beach. Small-boat anglers fishing marks in Cardigan Bay can expect tope, skate, conger, black bream, mackerel and flatfish.

Barmouth

From the shore angler's point of view, the estuary of the RIVER MAWDDACH offers the best opportunity of catching fish in the Barmouth area. Bass, flatfish, mullet and silver eels abound in the river-mouth area, and a leger baited with worm or crab bait will usually catch fish. Many of the flatfish tend to be on the small side, but on occasions it is possible to catch quite good-sized flounder from the Mawddach estuary.

Apart from the estuary itself, there is fair shore fishing

from the rocks opposite the coastguard station, YNYS-Y-BRAND ISLAND and the beach areas adjacent to Barmouth town. The quay at Barmouth is worth trying for mullet. From Barmouth right up the coast to PORT MADOC there is tremendous scope for beach fishing. Some good-sized bass and biggish tope have been caught in this area and a concentrated effort on the various beaches along this Merioneth coastline could produce surprise results.

Pwllheli

Beyond Pwllheli the long peninsula that faces out to BARDSAY SOUND and BARDSAY ISLAND offers magnificent scope for shore fishing. WHISTLING SANDS, MORFA NEFYN, HELL'S MOUTH, BORTH-Y-GEST, LLANBEDROG, ABERSOCH, GIMLET ROCK, LLANGIAN, ABERDARON and dozens of similar beach and rock marks are wide open for exploration. As might be expected from a rich stretch of coastline, this area produces a wider than normal range of fish species: pollack, pouting, cod, whiting, wrasse, bass, black bream, tope, conger, skate, mackerel, monkfish and a host of lesser species can be caught round the peninsula area. Offshore grounds are even richer—ling, shark, dogfish, gurnard and turbot can be added to the already impressive list of fish to be found in the area. Whether you like to float fish for mackerel, leger for tope or drift for shark, there is plenty of scope off this coastline. Local anglers use ABERSOCH BEACH as a bait larder, favourite local baits being razor fish, sand-eels and lugworms. Lugworm can be dug in local harbours.

Caernarvon

Situated on the Menai Straits, Caernarvon makes a good base for exploring the Straits area and Anglesey. At Caernarvon the SEINOT ESTUARY, DINAS BEACH and WATERLOO SHORE, ABER MENAI, CHURCH ISLAND, BEAUMARIS, GALLOWS POINT and BLACK POINT are the favoured local venues. For the pier enthusiast, the old wooden pier beside Caernarvon Docks, SEIONT HARBOUR, MENAI BRIDGE PIER and BANGOR PIER provide plenty of choice.

Fierce tides through the Menai Straits make fishing diffi-

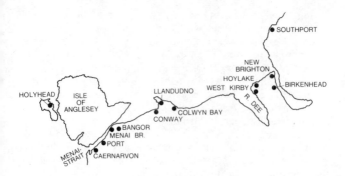

cult at times, but like most areas which are subjected to abnormally heavy runs of tide, the fishing in the MENAI STRAITS area is usually extremely good. Bass, tope and flatfish abound and at one time the black bream record was held by a fish caught in the Straits area.

Heavy leads are an essential part of Menai Straits fishing and correspondingly heavy beach-casting outfits also have to be employed. Peeler and soft-backed crab make the best general baits and can be found on most stretches of rocky foreshore. Lugworms can be dug in the VORYD ESTUARY. Ragworm are less common but can be dug in small quantities in Caernarvon Docks.

Anglesey

Beaches and rock marks all round the island provide a wealth of good fishing. HOLYHEAD and its adjacent area is well worth trying, favourite local spots being TREADDUR BAY, PENRHOS BEACH, SOUTH STACK, CHURCH BAY. On the other side of the island, RED WHARF BAY is well worth a visit.

Conway, Llandudno and Colwyn Bay

From Conway Sands round to the LITTLE ORMES HEAD and on to the sands of Colwyn Bay this interesting section of coastline offers a wide variety of good mixed shore and boat

89

fishing. BENARTH POINT, MORFA BEACH, BODLONDEB POINT, THE LITTLE ORME, RHOS POINT, PERMEAN HEAD and the COLWYN BAY SANDS are all good fishing venues. In between, many minor sections of shoreline are worth trying. This is mixed fishing, varying from vast expanses of flat, rather featureless sandy areas through to the rock fishing round the Little Ormes Head. Pollack, flatfish, bass, skate, conger, tope, dogfish and mackerel are regularly taken in their respective seasons. Pier enthusiasts have many places to try: LLANDUDNO PIER, the VICTORIA PIER at Colwyn Bay and various quays offer immense possibilities. Boat fishing in this entire area can be extremely rewarding; thornback skate and tope make up the bulk of the catches.

Rhyl and Prestatyn

Good shore fishing for various types of flatfish and first-class boat fishing make this area extremely popular. Rhyl is particularly noted for the quality of its offshore boat marks. Small boats operating along this coastline regularly bring in first-class catches of prime big thornback ray. Mackerel is the most favoured local boat-fishing bait. Fortunately these bait fish are usually common during the summer months, so fresh bait is seldom a problem.

Having read a great deal about the big catches of thornback ray caught off Rhyl, I decided to go to Wales to try for myself. On arrival I arranged to fit in with a charter party and soon we were anchored out over one of the local hot-spots. On the echo-sounder the bottom did not appear to be very interesting. Knowing thornback skate, however, I was not too worried by the featureless nature of the ground. On the way out we had feathered a fair number of mackerel for bait. Now with my 6–0 hook baited with a fresh fillet I settled back to fish hard and watch the other anglers in action. First fish in the boat was a splendid tope. Then I got a good-sized thornback. My catch seemed to trigger off a feeding frenzy among the resident skate population. Several times we had two or three good fish on at a time and the gaffman was kept solidly on the run. Finally it was over and time to take stock of the catch. In all we brought in nineteen good-sized thornback. We had also caught and released half a dozen or more undersized skate, two nice tope and numerous lesser-spotted dogfish. Rhyl had more than lived up to its reputation and I was satisfied and delighted with both the size and numbers of fish caught. This whole coastline is still drastically underfished. Only a few charter boats and privately-operated craft fish this coastline and obviously they do not begin to exhaust the offshore fishing. This area is wide open for thorough exploration and recommended to any British angler, particularly those who trail their own boats.

The Wirral

NEW BRIGHTON, WEST KIRBY and THURSTASTON all provide fishing possibilities. However, the whole of the area is rather dangerous, and most local anglers prefer to travel away from the Wirral to more convenient and productive venues.

Southport, Blackpool, Fleetwood, Morecambe Bay and Barrow-in-Furness

From Southport right up to Barrow-in-Furness, the whole coastline is made up of flat sand/mud beaches. Piers are plentiful and although the fishing is not generally very exciting, there is plenty of scope for experiment.

Southport

Flounder, dab and small plaice make up the bulk of summer catches. During the winter, whiting and the occasional cod are all that can be really expected. Offshore marks produce skate, tope, dogfish, mackerel, cod and whiting. Shore-fishing marks in the Southport area are the beach at FORMBY, SOUTHPORT BEACH and the PINFOLD CHANNEL. Pier anglers can pay Southport Corporation the modest sum of £1.00 for a season/day/night ticket to fish Southport Pier.

Blackpool

Summertime beach fishing on any of the beaches in the Blackpool area is out of the question. At night, it is sometimes possible to find an isolated spot, but even then crowds tend to spill off the promenade to make fishing something of a nightmare.

For summertime sport the estuaries of the RIVER RIBBLE and RIVER WYRE provide the best chance of escaping the holiday crowds. In winter, things are different and then it is worth fishing the local beaches. The same applies to pier and promenade fishing. LYTHAM ST ANNE'S promenade and the sea wall at Blackpool are then worth trying. The NORTH PIER at Blackpool can also be fairly good to fish from. This pier costs a few pence per day but gives the angler the chance of a good-sized winter cod or some whiting. Blackpool cod seldom reach a weight of more than 15 lb but the fish that are caught are all decent sizes, averaging 6 lb to 10 lb.

Cleveleys

Situated midway between Blackpool and Fleetwood, Cleveleys offers fair sport with flatfish, whiting and cod.

CLEVELEYS BREAKWATER and the promenade at ANCHORS-HOLME are the most productive spots to fish.

Fleetwood

Noted mainly as a commercial fishing port, Fleetwood has quite a lot to offer the angler as well. Charter boats can be hired from this port and it is possible to launch small boats as well. Boat marks produce cod, skate, dogfish, whiting, silver eels and flatfish. The occasional tope and conger eel may also be encountered. Shore fishermen can fish from EASTON BEACH, MARINE BEACH and from various points in the estuary of the River Wyre. Fleetwood Town Pier is also worth a try, as too is the Jubilee Quay in the area between the ferry and the fish dock.

The docks and the estuary are good for flatfish, particularly flounders and silver eels. Local beaches and the pier produce more of a mixed bag—cod, whiting, flatfish, eels, dogfish and the very occasional bass. Lugworm is a favourite local bait and can be dug from Marine Beach. Soft-back and peeler crabs make a good all-round bait in this area. These can be found round the wall of the Jubilee Quay.

Morecambe and Heysham

During the past few seasons Morecambe Bay has been much in the angling newspapers, with catch after catch of very big thornback ray. Local charter and private boats fishing various marks within the bay continually make contact with packs of heavyweight thornbacks, most of which fall to mackerel bait. Individual boat catches of up to twenty big ray in a single day's fishing are commonplace and a number of fish in excess of 20 lb have been taken.

The interesting thing is that for many years local anglers thought that Morecambe Bay had been fished out by commercial boats; then by accident someone made a big catch of skate and this set off a new school of thought. The result of this first catch has been an upsurge of interest and the establishment of Morecambe Bay as a productive fishing area. Shore anglers have always enjoyed fair beach and pier fishing in this area and this coupled with the good boat fishing has made the Morecambe area most popular.

All the local beaches are worth trying, as too are the outfall-pipe area, the sea wall, the BATTERY SLIPWAY and the CENTRAL PIER. Lugworm can be dug in the area. Flatfish, mostly dabs, flounders and small plaice, make up the bulk of the beach catches, but there is always the chance of making contact with the odd bass and, in the winter, whiting.

Barrow-in-Furness

Between Morecambe and Barrow there are many places where fishing is possible and anglers keen on flatfish will do well to explore this very tidal stretch of coastline. Barrow itself offers reasonably good fishing for flatfish, silver eels, pouting, cod, mackerel, bass and mullet.

Some of the best fishing in the area is round the ROA ISLAND HOTEL and the Causeway at FOULNEY ISLAND. The stone jetty directly oposite the Roa Island Hotel fishes well for good-sized cod and whiting. The occasional tope and bass can also be expected, but both are far from common. Between Barrow and Whitehaven miles of flat sand offers plenty of scope for exploration, particularly for flatfish.

Whitehaven

In my opinion Whitehaven is the start of true cod country, Along this stretch of coastline, with mixed rock and beach fishing available, anglers have plenty of scope for good mixed fishing. The WEST PIER and NORTH PIER, local names for the harbour walls at Whitehaven, provide fair fishing for flatfish, silver eels, pouting and the occasional mackerel. WELLINGTON BEACH is a fair flatfish and silver eel mark and the rocks at ST BEES HEAD are likely to produce all kinds of fish including cod and whiting. The cliff paths down to these rocks tend to be dangerous in wet weather and at night, so great care should be exercised when fishing this area. At PARTON there is also some fair rock fishing but on flood tides these rocks can become very dangerous so keep a weather eye on the tide and move inshore before it rises and cuts you off from safety.

It is sometimes possible to gather crabs for bait at Parton Rocks. Lugworm, however, is scarce and has to be bought locally or dug farther up the coast at Workington.

Workington

Workington town beach seldom fishes well, but HARRINGTON BEACH, to the south of the town and SIDDICK BEACH to the north are well worth visiting. These beaches fish best for flounder, dab and small plaice. Boat fishing along this coast can be very good, and boats can be launched at Harrington. The best fishing seems to be one to three miles offshore. Catches include skate, cod, whiting, dogfish and mackerel. Baited feathers are good for most species, although the skate are best fished with a plain running leger.

Maryport to Gretna Green

From Maryport to Gretna the fishing is mainly over flat sand and mud. At Maryport itself the promenade beach, GRASSLOT BEACH and the SOUTH and NORTH PIER are worth trying. Pollack, codling and flatfish are the common species. Boats can be launched at Maryport and the offshore fishing is good. Ragworm can be dug in many places. To the north of Maryport the coastline faces bleakly out on to the wastes of the Solway Firth. Various points along this coastline are fishable and creeks which wind inshore often produce good catches of prime flounders.

CHAPTER 6

The Isle of Man

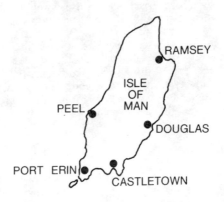

Virtually unexplored as an angling centre, the rocky coastline of the Isle of Man is only really fished by a handful of local enthusiasts.

The island has a tremendous amount of potential and can offer both the shore and boat angler an incredible variety of sizeable fish on a year-round basis. Probably the best fishing months are between June and October, although winter fishing for cod and big coalfish can be very productive. Favourite local species are pollack and haddock, but mackerel, wrasse, flatfish, skate, tope, dogfish, conger and possibly even big shark can be found round the island, giving every angler ample scope for experiment.

Peel

PEEL BREAKWATER has a justifiably good reputation for producing a seemingly endless stream of big fish. During the summer months shoals of extremely large mackerel abound in this area and pier anglers using float tackle or feathers regularly account for mackerel of 3 lb or more. It was off this breakwater that angler Peter Porter caught a mackerel of 4 lb 0½ oz. This huge fish held the record for the species for many years. Coalfish, pollack and wrasse can also be caught from the breakwater and anglers float fishing with worm or fish-strip baits often hook coalfish, known locally as 'blockan', of over 7 lb. Fish of this size hooked on light tackle put up a magnificent battle before they are ready for the drop net.

For the boat angler interested in haddock, a mark four miles west of the Peel breakwater can produce incredible catches of good-sized fish. Many boats have returned to port with over 50 stone of prime haddock aboard and these fish, with the occasional big cod, are enough to satisfy any angler.

Port St Mary

Tucked away in the corner of Port St Mary Bay and shielded from much of the weather by SPANISH HEAD this venue provides excellent fishing. The local breakwater has a good reputation for conger fishing, with individual fish of up to 30 lb being caught. When I was last in Port St Mary, anglers were being broken up fairly regularly by big congers and the usual stories of 60-lb and even 80-lb eels were circulating. This area produces most of the other local species and is particularly good for big dabs. Shore anglers and boat anglers alike specialise in dab-fishing sessions and it is not always the boats that get the biggest fish.

Beyond Spanish Head on the southern-most tip of the island is a small island known as the CALF OF MAN. This is separated from the mainland by Calf Sound. Virtually impossible to fish during a raging spring tide, Calf Sound can produce excellent pollack catches at slack water or during neap tides. Individual fish of 10 lb or more have been taken from this narrow neck of water and this is the ideal place for the angler interested in catching a big pollack. Bottom fishing from the rocks in this area can be good. The sandy gullies between the rocks are often thick with good-sized thornback ray and a big fish bait legered on the bottom of one of these natural roadways will usually pick up a good specimen or two.

Spanish Head itself fishes well for mackerel and pollack which can be readily caught on spinning baits or float-fished worm or fish-strip baits. Anglers interested in wrasse fishing will find this area particularly good, although it rarely produces any really hefty specimens.

Douglas

For the angler who is not inclined to travel far for his fishing or those who do not enjoy scrambling over rocks or sitting in boats, the VICTORIA PIER at Douglas is well worth a visit. This is a good pier for flatfishing and in past years has yielded some good catches of dabs and lemon sole, including one monster lemon sole of 2 lb 2 oz. Ragworms are the favourite bait on this pier; they can be dug from the beaches at Douglas, Castletown and Peel.

Basically the whole coast of the Isle of Man is more than capable of providing the shore or boat angler with good catches. From this point of view, many of the more out-of-the-way rock marks and beaches are worth a try, for if the main venues fish well, then the unfished marks should prove highly productive.

Tackle and Tips

Apart from conger fishing from the breakwaters, which obviously calls for heavy gear, most of the Isle of Man marks can be fished with comparatively light tackle. For spinning and float fishing for pollack, coalfish, mackerel, etc., a basic spinning rod and fixed-spool reel will suffice. This same outfit can also be used for flatfish and wrasse.

Boat anglers certainly do not need any specialised tackle. For spinning, red-gill eels, Toby spoons or heavy German sprats make the best lures.

For bottom fishing, particularly when boat fishing for haddock, small scallops, known locally as 'queenies', make the best bait, and are best fished on light paternoster or running leger tackle.

CHAPTER 7

Northern Ireland

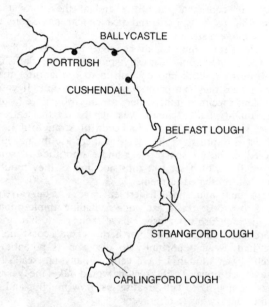

Northern Ireland is the untapped sea-angling El Dorado of the North, a gold mine of sea fishing whose rich potential is waiting to be discovered. With an arm of the Gulf Stream to keep water temperatures fairly high throughout the year, Northern Ireland provides good fishing at almost any time. From the rocky cliffs of the Causeway Coast to the peaceful

99

sea loughs of County Down there is wonderfully varied fishing. Every angler stands a chance of hooking a new British record each time he casts a bait in to the deep, clear waters. Here the fish run big and powerful, giving a wide selection of fine fishing far and away better than almost anywhere else in Europe. The most important species are skate, tope, haddock and cod. Halibut and shark have yet to be caught in consistent quantities and at the moment it is impossible to draw hard and fast conclusions about their precise movements.

There is something for every angler: baskets of fine, fat cod and prime haddock, greedy spurdog, plump flatfish and rod-bending pollack and coalfish in such quantities that in many places they can be hooked three at a time. If you are an ardent specimen hunter there are big fish galore to tempt you: mighty halibut in the vast depths off the Causeway Coast, vast skate and tope in beautiful Strangford Lough. The list is impressive: to add to it there are the newly discovered porbeagle shark packs and a multitude of smaller bottom fish which set rod tops nodding as they mouth at every bait presented to them.

Both boat and shore fishermen have a wide variety of marks to choose from, each one providing ample opportunity to catch fish after fish. I have spent many happy days ashore and afloat all round Northern Ireland's coastline, and have had every opportunity to discover its potential for myself. Even though I have caught many big sea fish on these expeditions, I still feel it would take me years of intensive angling to fully realise just how much grand fishing the country has to offer.

To help you get the best out of your sea angling in Northern Ireland, I have described each area in some detail, so that you can choose your venue to fit in with the fish you want to catch.

The Causeway Coast

Strictly speaking, the Causeway Coast stretches from MAGILLIGAN STRAND round to CUSHENDALL, and takes in PORTRUSH and BALLYCASTLE plus a host of tiny fishing villages.

Portrush is the main boat-fishing centre for the area and

boats leave this port daily to fish the famed CAUSEWAY BANK and the SKERRY ROCKS. Fishing here is for cod, large haddock, skate, spurdog, pollack, coalfish, mackerel and a wide variety of flatfish.

Haddock take pride of place along this particular section of the Causeway Coast: it was from Portrush and PORTSTEWART that 255 Irish specimen haddock were caught and recorded in 1968. You can also hook several species of gurnard here, with conger and very large ballan wrasse off the Skerry Islands. Tope occasionally turn up on the offshore grounds, and in 1971 at least three porbeagle shark were brought to gaff over the Causeway itself. Although this coast is not really noted for big common skate, quite a few of these monsters have been caught during the past few years and some hard fishing with big baits could produce some really hefty fish.

There is plenty of good shore fishing here, too, and the main species are pollack, coalfish, conger and wrasse. Magilligan Strand, near Londonderry, is famous for its bass in late autumn. Fish up to 12 lb are taken, and there are bass off the CASTLEROCK and Portstewart beaches: few local anglers try for them seriously.

Ballycastle

Although there is no proper harbour at Ballycastle, there is a serviceable jetty where during the summer a number of boats take out sea anglers. Most of these boats fish in Ballycastle Bay itself or around the magnificent cliffs on RATHLIN ISLAND, directly opposite Ballycastle Town. The bay has a wide variety of fish, including conger, cod, haddock, pollack, coalfish, dogfish, mackerel and thornback ray.

Common skate of 120 lb have been boated here. Much of the fishing around Rathlin is totally unexplored, and this is particularly true of the north side of the island where the water goes down to 133 fathoms. Huge halibut are known to exist over a number of marks round the island, and they have often been hooked, but in most cases they are lost before they can be gaffed.

Finally, there is quite good beach fishing at Ballycastle, not only for flatfish, but also for the occasional bass, ray and cod.

Ballycastle to Cushendall

At present there are no harbours suitable for charter-boat work along this section of the Antrim coast. Despite this the whole area is a shore fisherman's paradise. Spots to head for are the rock marks of MURLOUGH BAY and TORR HEAD. Both spots fish well for pollack, coalfish, rock cod and wrasse, and there are conger wherever there are rocks.

At CUSHENDUN, a nice sandy beach sheltered from prevailing winds gives you plenty of opportunity to try your luck with the flatfish. At Cushendall, RED BAY is a good place to try for skate and flatfish.

A tip: both areas fish best in the late evening.

Belfast Lough to Bangor

Despite heavy shipping, Belfast Lough can provide some first-rate fishing, particularly if you are new to sea angling and want to take things fairly easy.

Bangor is the ideal centre for boat fishing, its sheltered quays giving easy access to boats which can be out on the main fishing grounds very quickly.

The lough is best known for its skate and cod. Thornback and cuckoo rays are plentiful and bait is never a problem, as the lough is usually full of fine big mackerel. At the mouth of the lough, near COPELAND ISLAND, LIGHTHOUSE ISLAND and MEW ISLAND, there is good mixed fishing for a wide variety of bottom fish. Catches are mostly of cod, whiting and skate, but very big hake are sometimes brought up from deeper water.

Donaghadee

Boats are usually available from this sheltered and pleasant harbour. The main sport is for coalfish and pollack. From the shore here it is possible to catch plenty of medium-sized flatfish and worm bait is easy to dig.

Strangford Lough

Strangford Lough is without doubt one of the finest big fish venues in the British Isles. If you are a dedicated sea-specimen hunter interested in 'ton up' skate and really large tope, Strangford must rate right at the top of your list: and ninety per cent of it is quite unexplored and unexploited. Common skate of over 100 lb are so common that local boatmen now release any fish under this weight. You can hire your boat at Portaferry Quay. Bait is problem here. Big mackerel shoals are common in summer, and lug and ragworm can be dug around the lough shore.

The largest rod-caught skate yet to come from Strangford Lough weighed in at an incredible 187 lb. Caught in 1969, it still stands as the biggest skate yet taken from the lough. It was a monster, but only a medium-sized fish in comparison to some of the giants there must be here.

Very large tope are common, and individual specimens to 60 lb have been boated. In one month alone, five tope of over 50 lb were recorded from the lough, which must make Strangford Britain's top big-tope water. Apart from skate and tope, there are flatfish, thornback ray, pollack, coalfish, mullet, very large spurdog, wrasse and the occasional herring shoal in winter.

A wreck just above PORTAFERRY holds some good-sized conger but they are rarely fished for.

In the open sea outside the entrance to the lough there is good mixed fishing for a wide variety of bottom fish. Large cod are commonplace, and pollack, dogfish, small skate, and gurnard can be taken in quantity.

Carlingford Lough

This calm, warm lough in County Down is as typical of Northern Ireland's sea fishing grounds as Strangford—full of fish and rarely visited. Again, there is a wide variety of fish. A day out will probably see you bring in spurdog, haddock and small cod—plus a medium-sized skate or tope.

Spurdog are the ruling species here, and it is often difficult to get a bait through the thick shoals without first having to retrieve line and shake three or four of them off. (Recently a local angler complained that during a competition he had half a ton of spurdog and did not even figure in the result list.)

No big skate have been taken, but this is most likely because the lough is still grossly underfished. It would probably give a monster or two to the angler prepared to take it seriously.

Immediately outside the lough there are plenty of average-sized cod in winter. The lough shores make fine marks for rock fishing, and the beaches at CRANFIELD POINT and GREENCASTLE are well known for fine cod.

Ragworm, lugworm and sand-eel are there for the digging on the shores of the lough.

Shore fishing

Good shore fishing is available at almost any point round Northern Ireland's coasts. Because of this you will have ample opportunity to fish to your heart's content without ever having to go out to sea, for shore angling is so far totally undeveloped.

Big pollack and coalfish, locally called *lythe* as they are in Scotland, are very common wherever there are rocky outcrops surrounded by deep water.

Where headlands jut out into sandy sea beds, skate and ray can be caught in good numbers. They are the main species, but there are also wrasse, conger, gurnard, small plaice, flounders, dogfish, mackerel and whiting. I believe it might well be possible to catch tope from the shore as well, particularly off the Antrim Coast.

Tackle

Choice of tackle for use in Northern Ireland's waters depends a great deal on the kind of fishing you intend to indulge in.

To be ready for everything I suggest you carry a selection of four outfits to cover all aspects of boat and shore fishing. Obviously the four outfits mentioned are open to change, and as every angler has his own ideas on tackle, they can be switched according to preference.

For the heavyweight species like shark, big common skate and halibut, you should use a heavy rod with a test curve of at least 50 lb. This rod can be balanced with a 6–0, or better still 9–0, multiplier fully loaded with 80 lb to 100 lb braided terylene or dacron line.

For smaller species, including tope, use a more sporting outfit, such as a medium-weight boat rod and 4–0 multiplying reel. Remember that there is little shallow water available and on average you will fish into something like 30 or 40 fathoms of water. Because of their low line-carrying capacity, reels below 4–0 size are not advisable for boat fishing.

For shore work, a 4- to 6-oz beach-caster, coupled with a large capacity fixed-spool or beach-casting multiplier, is the ideal outfit. For all-round work this should be used in conjunction with a line of between 22 to 25 lb.

Finally, if you are after pollack and coalfish from the rocks, use a light spinning rod roughly 8 or 9 ft long. You can use this either with a small multiplier or medium-sized fixed-spool reel.

Always carry a wide selection of terminal tackle, lures, hooks, swivels and leads, for although there are good tackle shops in Northern Ireland they are widely spaced and it is possible to run out of some essential terminal gear which may be impossible to replace easily.

Always carry a couple of spare rod rings and a reel of whipping silk, so that you can replace a cracked or damaged ring easily and quickly.

Tackle rigs (artificial)

Jig baits, tandem spoon rigs and feathers are the local anglers' terminal tackle. These are all excellent catchers, and can be used for cod, whiting, haddock, gurnard, pollack, pouting, ling and mackerel. All artificial lures can be improved by baiting the hooks with fish, squid, or octopus cuttings.

Rubber eels of the 'Red-gill' variety are deadly, particularly when used from the shore for pollack and coalfish.

For drift fishing for cod and most bottom fish you can use nylon paternoster to good effect. Hook sizes should vary between 3–0 and 6–0, depending on the size of fish you are after and the bait you are using.

When fishing at anchor for big tope or skate, use a plain running leger. A wire trace is essential, and for tope this should have a breaking strain of around 45 lb. However, for big skate, a trace with a breaking strain of at least 100 lb is essential. The lead should be allowed to run on a Kilmore or Clements boom. Always use a big swivel to connect the trace to the reel line. For tope, use an 8–0 hook, for skate a 10–0 or 12–0 size.

CHAPTER 8

West Coast of Scotland

The west coast of Scotland and its adjacent islands probably provides some of the best sea-fishing potential in Great Britain. The entire west coast is rich in fish of many species and to anglers who are prepared to travel, and if necessary to rough it, in search of first-class sport, the west coast of Scotland, with its magnificent scenery and numerous isolated stretches of virtually unfished coastline, offers something for everyone.

The Highlands are still sparsely populated, so that in many highly suitable areas boat fishing is either an impossibility or at best is severely restricted through lack of boats and boatmen. Even in ports where charter-boat facilities are available Sunday fishing is seldom practised. Even Scottish commercial fishermen don't work on Sundays and very few charter-boat skippers are prepared to break long-established traditions. But the Highlands and Islands Development Board is now taking steps to develop fully many ports and charter-boat enterprises. Grants are being provided to suitable firms and the future charter-boat situation looks extremely rosy. Although developments of this kind obviously take time and preparation, from talks that I have had with development board officials I am certain that the boat situation is going to improve rapidly during the next few seasons. Once reliable charter boats are available in all areas then the 'sky is the limit'—for the west coast of Scotland is capable of yielding individual fish and mass catches that will tumble existing records and make angling

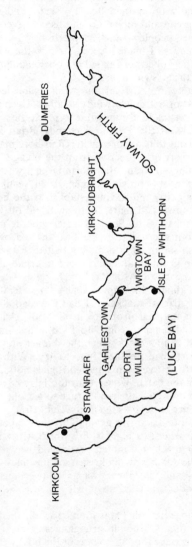

news. One such charter-boat enterprise is already established at Tobermory on the Isle of Mull and in its first season this boat continually brought in 'ton-up' skate, and mammoth catches of big cod and mixed ground-fish. I never believe in accepting other people's word on the fishing potential of a new ground and so I made a special trip to the Isle of Mull to fish from the Tobermory-based boat belonging to charter-boat skipper Brian Swinbanks.

Unfortunately my arrival on Mull coincided with a lengthy period of extremely windy weather. Despite the fact that the weather made it impossible to reach the magnificent fishing grounds off the Treshnish Islands, Brian Swinbanks decided to go out to fish more sheltered inshore marks which gave us some sort of protection from the savage winds that came screaming in from the storm-lashed wastes of the Atlantic. Like most Scottish boatmen, Brian Swinbanks likes to fish on the drift, and having established the boat's position over a known cod mark Brian switched off the engine and we began to fish. Seconds after our terminal rigs touched bottom every rod in the boat arched over as fish after hefty fish slammed into the big baited feathers.

'Cod,' Brian grunted, and who was I to argue as I fought my own private battle with the fish. Minutes later the cod were coming aboard in strings. Using three feathers, each baited with a strip of mackerel, I had three good-sized cod to show from my first drop down off Mull. I suppose we got a dozen cod ranging from 7 to 14 lb in the first minutes of fishing—all from a mark which the skipper only regarded as a last-resort, bad-weather spot to try. With the boat obviously drifting over a massed cod pack nobody wasted time admiring the catch, we were all too busy re-baiting the big white and orange feathers in a race to get our baits back to fish level. Sure enough as the lead weights touched bottom we all struck into good fish again. This time I got two and lost a baited feather to a big, fast fish which struck at around the mid-water mark. I doubted that a cod was responsible for ripping the feathered hook clear of the line—my guess was coalfish—and from the way it powerhoused down into deep water it was obviously in the heavyweight class.

Despite losing this fish I was more than satisfied with the brace of cod that I brought struggling and kicking to the surface. By this stage the fish pounds of the boat were rapidly filling, then as suddenly as the fish had come they were gone again, leaving us to drift on over an obviously fishless stretch of sea bed. Suddenly, however, the echo-sounder showed a steep rise on the sea bed, capped with a ridge of obviously rugged ground. Above the ridge a smudge of faint dots indicated a shoal of fish. Moments later our baits were dragging up the side of the bank and as they reached the peak of the ridge the fish hit us in waves. From their speed and spirit they obviously weren't cod: pollack or coalfish was the general opinion and as the first leash of fish broke surface the distinctive white lateral line showed them to be coalfish. Less tasty than cod, big coalfish are a solidly sporting species, full of fight and fire; they are more than capable of putting a boat rod through its paces and on this trip the fish were so concentrated that they were coming aboard in threes.

By the time we had re-baited we were beyond the bank and Brian decided to motor back uptide to start the whole drift again. Trying to put us back over the original cod hot-spot was far from easy, but he managed to achieve this objective quite easily and once again it was bait and drop, strike, and retrieve as each and every bait took fish. For a south-coast angler used to slow cod fishing the speed and intensity of this Mull-style codding was almost unbelievable. Then once again we were out of the shoaling ground—but at a conservative estimate, we had over 1,000 lb of beautiful cod aboard. On top of this we had coalfish, the odd pollack, and a few big red gurnard. Now with the wind rising steadily it was time to go, time for the long run back to port with green water breaking in a spray of icy mist across our bows. Time to talk, to think and to wonder at a fishing ground that could produce such a huge catch on a day which made it impossible to go out to the known top fishing marks of the rugged Treshnish Islands. This was solid proof of the kind of fishing the west coast of Scotland has to offer. In the near future, when charter boats and anglers appear in these waters in increasing numbers, catches will no doubt be made that will firmly establish the west coast of Scotland as the best sport-fishing ground anywhere around the British Isles.

Dumfries to Stranraer

Dumfries

Although far from being a good fishing venue, the Dumfries area does occasionally produce fair catches of flatfish, cod, whiting and the very occasional bass. The estuary of the RIVER NITH is a good place for flounders and silver eels and there is ample scope for shore fishing at many points along the coast between Dumfries and DALBEATTIE.

Wigtown Bay

From Kirkcudbright right round the bay to WHITHORN there is a tremendous variation of coastline which offers plenty of scope for both shore and boat fishing. BORNESS POINT, RAVENSHALL POINT, GARLIESTON, CAIRN HEAD and BURROW HEAD provide good mixed shore fishing for a wide range of fish. The rocky points fish well for dogfish, cod, pollack and similar rock-dwelling species, while the many sandy beaches and bays are ideal for flatfish catching.

Luce Bay

Long established as a top fishing spot, Luce Bay has a reputation for producing big fish of many kinds. Porbeagle shark have been caught here and the quality of the tope and skate fishing within the bay area has long been recognised as some of the best in the British Isles.

Luce Bay is named after the River Luce which rises to the west of Stranraer and enters the bay near GLENLUCE. In this corner of Luce Bay, big grey mullet abound and vast shoals of these shy-biting fish can often be encountered. Luce Bay sands are ideal for beach-casting, particularly for flatfish and the odd bass, and at SANDHEAD it is possible to launch small boats. Worm bait is easy to dig on the sands and an hour or so spent with a fork will normally turn up enough worms for a full day's fishing requirements. Good shore-fishing stations to head for are the Luce River estuary, TERRALLY BAY, MONRIETH and DRUMMORE. The whole of the MULL OF GALLOWAY is rich in good fishing. Spots like CLAN-

YARD BAY, HOLE STONE BAY, MONEY HEAD, PORTPATRICK and the entrance of LOCH RYAN can provide excellent catches of big fish, up to and including heavyweight conger and 20-lb-plus cod.

Stranraer

Known mostly as a ferry terminal, Stranraer, at the head of Loch Ryan, is quite a good place to fish. Conger, skate, tope, cod, haddock, whiting, mackerel and mullet are all common in the area. Basically sheltered, Loch Ryan makes a good boat-fishing centre with ample opportunity for launching small boats. The most popular shore-fishing stations are INNERMESSAN POINT, PORT BEG, CORSEWELL POINT, LADY BAY and FINNARTS BAY. From BALLANTRAE to AYR there is plenty of good rock and beach available. At GIRVAN, midway between the two towns, the town pier is good for mullet, mackerel, pollack and coalfish.

For shore fishermen HORSE ROCK is the best place.

Ayr to Oban

Ayr

Prolific fishing grounds either side of Ayr town make this a popular section of coastline with both shore and boat anglers alike. The rock marks at FISHERTON and HEADS OF AYR are good for cod, conger, pollack and coalfish. There is good fishing from Ayr Pier and in the harbours of Ayr and NEWTON.

Ardrossan

I have never found fishing at Ardrossan to be particularly good, although I understand that at times WINTON PIER, MONTGOMERY PIER and nearby SALTCOATS PIER fish quite well for coalfish and small cod. Beyond Ardrossan, miles of coastline are available to the angler—WEMYSS BAY and CUMBRAE ISLAND provide good mixed fishing with codling as the predominant species.

Gourock

The Gourock area is regarded as one of the best cod-fishing spots yet discovered round the coasts of the British Isles. Situated in the Firth of Clyde facing towards the mouths of GARE LOCH and LOCH LONG, Gourock makes an ideal base port from which to explore the fishing potential of this area.

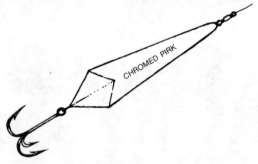

Fig. 12 Pirk bait.

For shore and pier fishermen CLOCH POINT, GREENOCK ESPLANADE, MCINROY'S POINT and Gourock Pier offer ample opportunity for good cod fishing, but the biggest cod fall to boat anglers. This is the area that produced two consecutive British cod records and could easily produce yet another. It was in the Firth of Clyde that jigging with heavy, chrome-plated pirk-style (see fig. 12) lures first became a firmly established method of catching Scottish cod. In its hey-day, the Firth of Clyde area probably produced more big cod than any other known mark off the British coastline, ninety per cent of these monster fish being taken on big pirk-style lures. Cod evidently come into this area to feed and spawn and when this was first discovered vast catches of fish weighing up to 46 lb each were taken.

Big, hungry cod will strike at anything that vaguely resembles food and the pirk baits used by local dinghy anglers seem to be just what the hunting cod look for. At times, the fishing was so good that bags of 400 to 500 lb of monstrous cod were regarded as no more than 'run of the mill' catches. Naturally, anglers from all over the country converged on this cod El Dorado and the area suffered from drastic over-fishing. Even so, good cod still abound in the Firth of Clyde and its adjoining lochs and even today individual fish of up to 30 lb are regarded as little more than fair, average specimens.

Strong tides and the fact that the cod shoals congregate in very small areas make this fishing difficult at times. However, local anglers are usually only too pleased to help visitors to the area and by asking for advice on the precise whereabouts of the best fishing, it is often possible to make good catches on your first outing.

Isle of Arran

Once justifiably famous for its haddock fishing, the Isle of Arran now seldom produces big 'haddie' in quantity. Even so fishing in LAMLASH BAY and BRODICK BAY is often productive. Cod, spurdog, mackerel, tope, small haddock and plaice are the most common species. Spurdog often turn up in vast packs and make a thorough nuisance of themselves by snatching at any natural or artificial bait that they see. They are good fun to catch but their claw-like dorsal spines

113

make them awkward fish to handle and their tendency to take any bait soon makes most anglers regard them as a pest. Once a spurdog pack goes on the feed it is possible to catch hundredweights of fish ranging from 7 lb to 14 lb each. The first time you make a big catch of ravenous spurdog you enjoy the experience, but once you realise the fish are suicidal, the enjoyment subsides and from that time on you will loathe the very sight of one of these voracious little sharks.

Shore fishing round Arran is generally very good indeed. CORRIE ROCKS and CLAUCHELANDS POINT are two popular stations but there are dozens of similar places to fish, all of which are well worth trying. Pollack, coalfish and small cod abound off the island, so there is plenty of scope for light-tackle tactics.

Oban

Although basically a commercial fishing port, Oban is also quite a good sport-fishing centre as well. Most of the fishing in this area is done from boats which mainly work marks in the vicinity of KERRERA ISLAND. These marks produce mackerel, skate, cod and the occasional big tope. Dogfish of various kinds often make a considerable nuisance of themselves, especially when fish-strip baits are being used.

Isle of Mull

Easily reached by hourly ferry service from Oban, the Isle of Mull is a first-class sea angling centre. Ample beach and rock marks provide good fishing stations for a wide variety of fish. The main road which circles this beautiful island gives easy access to many productive shore marks, and the varied nature of the island's coastline provides the opportunities to fish for a wide range of species.

Flatfish, mostly flounders, dabs and small plaice are common on all the sandy beaches round the island and beach-casting tackle with worm bait will normally produce good bags of medium-sized fish, particularly during a rising tide. Rock marks produce pollack, coalfish, mackerel and wrasse. Rocks close to sand are worth trying, for a big mackerel fillet cast out on to the sand will probably produce some fair bags or thornback skate.

Boat fishing off Mull is magnificent, although the weather can occasionally make life difficult. Cod are the most common species, although the various marks round the island have yielded numerous 100-lb-plus skate, and monster tope. TOBERMORY makes the best boat-fishing base, although small boats can be launched at many places round the island. For those anglers interested in game fish, it is often possible to make contact with sea trout by spinning directly off burn or river mouths. A small Mepps spoon or Toby lure is best for this style of angling.

Fort William to Cape Wrath

Between Oban and Fort William the coastline is indented by numerous sandy bays and rock-fishing marks. Most of these places fish well, particularly for codling, pollack, wrasse, dogfish and flatfish. There is good boat fishing in LOCH LINNHE although tides can make life difficult in this area. Big tope are known to frequent this loch.

Flatfish of many kinds are extremely common. LOCH LEVEN which opens off Loch Linnhe, provides top-quality, free sea-trout fishing. Worm bait is easy to dig on all local beaches and at Fort William there is some reasonable fishing to be had from local piers. At CORRAN near the Ballachulish Ferry there is good rock fishing, and pollack and sea trout are very common in this area. There is a wealth of undiscovered shore fishing all round ARDNAMURCHAN POINT. Wherever it is possible to get down safely to sea level, you will find plenty of small cod, wrasse, pollack, dogfish and flatfish all eagerly waiting to snap up your bait.

Kyle of Lochalsh

Basically one of the three ferry points for the Isle of Skye, the Kyle of Lochalsh provides magnificent shore fishing. At night the deep water round the jetty is worth fishing for conger and thornback skate are commonly caught at this point.

Rock and beach marks on either side of the Kyle produce the usual types of fish and also some hefty dogfish as well.

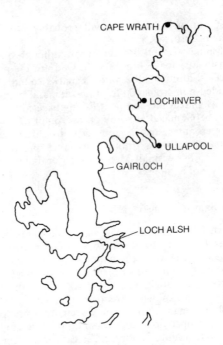

Bait is plentiful on all the local beaches and crab can be gathered round the rocks.

Boat fishing produces fine haddock, cod, conger, tope, skate and big mackerel. The coastline round LOCH CARRON and LOCH TORRIDON offers ample scope. Small boats can be launched in most areas and the offshore marks fish well.

Two- or three-hook paternoster tackle baited with worm, fish or mussel makes the best terminal rig. Medium-sized haddock are very common throughout the area and the paternoster can usually be relied upon to take plenty of these nice little fish. Small cod and flatfish will also fall to this rig.

Loch Gairloch

In recent years, Gairloch has become extremely popular with sea anglers. Gairloch Bay is particularly suited to boat fishing and marks round LONGA ISLAND at the northern entrance to the Bay fish extremely well. Skate, cod, haddock, tope, ling and the occasional turbot are the main species caught. Shore fishing produces flatfish, pollack, wrasse and dogfish.

Ullapool

Long established as a top fishing and holiday centre, Ullapool has in its time produced a multitude of monster skate. Over-exploitation has partially ruined the big skate fishing in this area, although the occasional big fish is still caught near the SUMMER ISLES or from marks round HORSE ISLAND. In my opinion, anglers visiting Ullapool should think more in terms of small-boat fishing, for LOCH BROOM is full of fish, most of which can be caught from open boats. For those anglers wishing to launch their own boat, there is ample beach space available. Rowing boats and self-drive motor-boats can also be hired from the beach. I have used these hire boats on many occasions and from them I have taken good catches of haddock, mackerel and flatfish, including the rare type known as *megrim*.

I usually fish light in Loch Broom, for I find a spinning rod is ideal for all the smaller species. For those anglers who would rather use standard boat-fishing tackle and big baits there are plenty of good-sized thornback ray and dogfish in Loch Broom. Tope may also be encountered.

Beyond Ullapool the rugged coastline is virtually unfished. I have tried rock fishing at many points and have invariably caught fish, nothing vast, just good average pollack, wrasse, codling and dogfish. At ACHILTIBUIE, a shore angler recently caught a 130-lb common skate while fishing from the harbour wall.

Lochinver

Between Ullapool and Lochinver lie hundreds of square miles of fishable coastline most of which has never been touched by anglers. This rugged country, which would take a lifetime to explore, is rich in good fishing. At Lochinver the harbour and beach fishes quite well but the best shore fishing in the area is from the rocky headlands on either side of the village.

Coalfish, pollack, mackerel, dogfish, codling and wrasse are the main species caught by shore anglers. There is not much boat fishing but specimen fish of many types can be caught from the various marks in the area.

Cape Wrath

Between Lochinver and Cape Wrath, the fishing is a totally unknown quality. I have tried shore fishing at various accessible points along this isolated stretch of magnificent coastline, mostly with reasonable results. For a 'get away from it all' camping-cum-fishing holiday, the Cape Wrath area would be hard to equal. Home to thousands of fascinating sea birds which gather to feed on the fish that frequent this area, Cape Wrath has much to interest the visitor. The only drawback to the extreme north of Scotland is the weather, which at best is uncertain. I have been to Cape Wrath and had a week of brilliant sunshine; another time it rained constantly.

Tackle Warning

The north of Scotland is a very underpopulated and underdeveloped area. Shops are scarce at best and north of Ullapool fishing tackle is practically unobtainable.

Owing to the rugged nature of this coastline, tackle losses during fishing are invariably high. To avoid losing valuable fishing time trying to replace lost tackle, it is advisable to carry a wide range of terminal tackle and spare spools of line at all times.

To cut costs and to avoid carrying tackle that you may never use, it is advisable to plan the contents of your tackle box carefully. For shore fishing from rocks stick to lightish tackle. A spinning outfit can be used for spinning, float fishing and light bottom fishing. Cheap lures are best, for heavy, weed-covered rock can claim a good many artificial baits during the course of a day. Fish do not care much for the cost of a lure, they are only interested in its appearance and a cheap, expendable spoon which cost half the price of a similar lure produced by a known company will usually catch just as many fish as its expensive counterpart. Float fishing is a good method to use, particularly for wrasse, coalfish and pollack.

Bottom fishing over sand is easy and seldom leads to lost tackle but it still pays to carry a good selection of beach-casting leads, various types and sizes of eyed hooks, swivels and so on. In Scottish waters, fish show a distinct liking for feathers and it pays to carry a dozen sets of mackerel or cod feathers. I normally buy six feather traces: I cut these in half, using only three feathers at a time, so by carrying a dozen full sets I end up with twenty-four three-feather traces. Usually this is enough for a fortnight's hard fishing.

CHAPTER 9

Hebrides, Orkney, and Shetland Islands

The Hebrides

Isle of Skye

With plenty of good, easily-accessible shore fishing available and the possibility of hiring or launching boats, the Isle of Skye offers excellent fishing to the visiting angler. Pollack, coalfish, wrasse, dogfish, tope, skate, conger, mackerel, cod, haddock and several kinds of flatfish are common. Shore fishing with conventional beach-casting tackle will produce good results at almost any point round the island, and for the light-tackle enthusiast, spin fishing from the rock marks will provide fabulous sport with pollack, coalfish and big mackerel.

Isle of Lewis

STORNOWAY is the main fishing centre on the Isle of Lewis. From this port charter boats operate to take anglers from all over Great Britain and Europe out to the deep-water skate, tope, and mixed fishing grounds.

Like all the islands in the Hebrides, Lewis has plenty to offer the shore angler. Flatfish abound in sandy and gravelly areas and a one- or two-hook running leger, incorporating long-shanked flatfish hooks baited with worm, will usually produce a good selection of flounders, dabs, plaice and even megrim.

Other islands

More or less unexplored from an angling point of view, all the islands in the Hebrides are more than capable of providing first-class shore and boat fishing. To get the best out of any of the islands it pays to be a versatile angler, changing styles to suit local conditions and the habits of local fish. Spin or float fish from the rocks, beach-cast over sandy ground and try jigging, feathering or bottom fishing from a boat. The mixed fish stocks off the Scottish islands provide such a wide variety of angling opportunities that it pays handsomely to exploit each possibility to the full.

Spinning is a favourite method of mine. It is a clean, easy style of angling that allows me to travel light, cover plenty of ground and catch a reasonable variety of fish during the course of an average day's sport. For this style of angling I limit myself as far as bait choice is concerned for it is easy to overspend on lures, most of which are designed to catch the angler rather than the fish. I normally carry a dozen lures of the German sprat, Abu Costa type. To allow for all tidal conditions I mix the sizes so that I can change weights rather than style of lure to fit in with prevailing conditions. My whole lure selection fits into a small flat pocket-sized tin. Armed with this, a rod, reel, landing net and a small selection of snap swivels, I am free to wander at will from rock gully to rock gully, thoroughly covering each possible fish lie as I go. If I run into biggish pollack or coalfish, I use a fairly large lure, if the mackerel shoal are within casting range, I switch to a smaller bait.

Orkney and the Shetland Islands

The islands of Orkney and Shetland undoubtedly provide some of the most exciting boat fishing to be found anywhere round the coast of Great Britain. This is mixed fishing at its best. Big, small and medium-sized fish abound and even the first-time angler can go to sea off these lovely islands and come back with a mammoth catch at the end of the day.

If you want a monster skate or halibut, these are the islands to head for. If, on the other hand, you just want to catch good fish in quantity, then make up a terminal rig which incorporates three big white or orange cod feathers, bait each feather with a strip of mackerel, lower the triple feather rig to the bottom and hang on tight. Cod, ling, pollack, whiting and even haddock abound in such quantity that you can hardly get the tackle down to sea-bed level before your rod top starts to twitch and dip to the tugging, determined bites of hungry fish.

The last time I fished Orkney was during a three-day boat-fishing festival. Terrible weather limited our choice of fishing localities. Even so, thousands of pounds of fish were landed daily. Mostly cod, ling and pollack, fish averaging between 4 lb and 10 lb with here and there a 20-lb cod or ling to add interest to the catch. If conditions had been better we would have fished more productive grounds still. While we were fishing in the PENTLAND FIRTH, one boat stayed inside to fish the sheltered waters of SCAPA FLOW in

Fig. 13   Halibut rig, incorporating a bar spoon and a wobbling spoon.

the hope of a big skate. Their tactics worked and they took fish to 140 lb. Small by Orkney and Shetland standards maybe, but monsters as far as the rest of the country was concerned.

Orkney

Most boat fishing in this area is done either in Scapa Flow itself or in the Pentland Firth. The west face of HOY ISLAND is a favourite venue, particularly if you want to catch a halibut. The wild waters of Pentland hold a good head of these monstrous, predatory flatfish. Halibut use the Pentland Firth as a well-stocked larder, feeding indiscriminately on cod, ling, pollack and coalfish.

Most successful halibut fishermen use a particular style of baited-spoon rig which incorporates an elongated silver

122

spoon (see fig. 13). The hook that trails beyond this spoon is baited with a whole fillet of fresh mackerel. Mackerel used either whole or in fillets is also widely used as bait for the giant skate of Scapa Flow. Commercial boats have taken fish from this World War I shipping graveyard to weights in excess of 300 lb. Boat marks round Orkney are legion. Favourite hot-spots are COSTA HEAD, MARWICK HEAD, EDAY FIRTH, STRONSAY FIRTH and the BROUGH OF BIRSAY.

From the shore angler's point of view Orkney is an undiscovered treasure-house of fishing potential. Sandy beaches and rocky headlands abound. Each section of the island's coastline is more than capable of providing good sport. Coalfish, pollack and flatfish are numerous and mackerel can be caught in many places. Conger can be taken from deep water adjacent to rocky outcrops and from the wartime CHURCHILL BARRIERS built by Italian prisoners of war it is possible to drop a big bait into deep water and catch skate and conger. All in all, Orkney is an unexploited shore angler's paradise for unlike boat fishing which is only possible in reasonable weather, the shore angler can always tuck himself away out of the wind in a sheltered spot on one side of the islands.

Quite apart from bottom fishing it is also good fun float fishing round Orkney's rocks and barriers. A bait suspended off the bottom in this way seems to be very attractive to coalfish and pollack, both of which reach a good size in Orcadian waters. Spinning with an elongated wobbling spoon is also great fun; again coalfish and pollack are the main species caught but in some areas it is also easy to catch vast numbers of big northern mackerel.

The Shetland Islands

Even less exploited than Orkney, the sport-fishing potential of the Shetlands remains unexplored.

During the four months between June and September 1970 for example, 94 skate weighing over 100 lb each were caught in Shetland waters. In 1971, during a skate championship, seventeen skate of over 100 lb were weighed in. It was in Shetland that Mr R. MacPherson caught his record-breaking 226½-lb monster which broke both the British and European record for the species. Much bigger skate are known to exist in the waters round these islands and it can only be a matter of time before this record is broken by a bigger and better fish.

Shetlanders are jealous of their fishing and are wisely making every attempt to conserve big skate stocks for future generations of anglers. This catch, weigh and return policy is most admirable. Big skate have little value other than as sport fish, consequently a well-conceived and executed conservation plan shows an intelligent regard for the safety of a particular species of large fish. If other areas had followed this policy in earlier years, big skate would now be much more common than they are.

Apart from its magnificent skate fishing, Shetland, like Orkney, is rich in fish of many types. Gigantic halibut, big cod, ling, haddock and flatfish abound, giving ample opportunity for all kinds of fishing activity. Shore fishing as such is not practised, although like Orkney there are a multitude of fishable spots. No doubt in years to come anglers will gradually discover the shore-fishing potential of Shetland and when this occurs I am certain that many big catches of large fish will be made. All this is in the future. At present Shetland is wide open, waiting for a group of enterprising shore fishermen to exploit its possibilities to the full.

CHAPTER 10

East Coast of Scotland

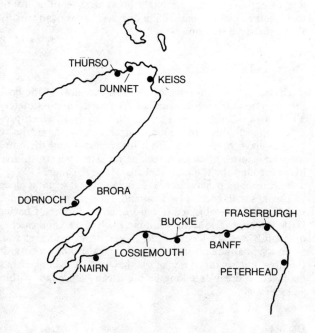

Caithness to Nairn

Facing out directly on to the productive waters of the
PENTLAND FIRTH, Caithness has built up a reputation for
being one of the premier boat-fishing areas in Scotland.

Famous for its monster halibut, Caithness has probably produced more of these giant flatfish than any other venue in the British Isles. Halibut apart, the rich waters of Caithness produce immense catches of cod, ling, pollack, coalfish and a host of smaller species as well. For example, during the 1971 European Championships no less than 25,000 lb of sizeable fish were weighed in. With over 100 miles of coastline to explore, Caithness has a great deal to offer, for if bad weather makes boat fishing impossible, you can usually find a sheltered shore-mark to fish.

Thurso and Scrabster

Thurso is the main town of the area but most of the boat fishing is done from Scrabster, a port situated approximately a mile away. Scrabster has an excellent harbour which provides opportunities for good conger fishing. Some hefty congers have been caught from this harbour and there are the usual stories of tackle-wrecking monsters which still live in and around the foundation walls of the harbour.

Boat fishing off Scrabster is first-class, but it is not a place to use a small boat. The Pentland Firth is a treacherous stretch of water subjected to hard tides at all times. Charter boats working various marks in the Firth make good catches of dogfish, cod, haddock, skate, ling, flatfish, mackerel and, of course, halibut. Porbeagle shark are also known to visit the area but so far every shark that has been hooked has managed to break free long before it can be brought within gaffing range.

Dunnet

Eight miles east of Thurso, Dunnet lies at the end of the two-and-a-half-mile-long beach known as DUNNET SANDS. This is a good beach for digging worm bait and for catching flatfish and several small bass have been caught.

Keiss

Between JOHN O'GROATS and WICK the small fishing village of Keiss provides ample opportunity for rock fishing and

126

there are some big plaice to be had at SINCLAIR'S BAY. Many rock fishermen spin for mackerel in this area and it is common to get into a good-sized sea trout while fishing in this way.

Sutherland

South of WICK the coastline becomes gradually less rugged. Sandy bays are common and there is plenty of opportunity for shore fishing.

Brora

This small harbour town boasts a few charter boats and it is possible to launch small boats in the harbour area. Cod, ling, skate and conger eels are the main species caught from boats. Flatfish, pollack and mackerel are common on the shore marks.

Dornoch to Inverness

Dornoch gives good access to the northern fishing banks in the DORNOCH FIRTH. At nearby EMBO there is fair rock fishing and EMBO PIER is worth trying. Boat trips are difficult to arrange in the Dornoch area although there is a great deal of scope for boat fishing on this section of coastline, cod and good-sized flatfish being the most common species encountered.

Nairn to Dundee
Nairn

Situated on the MORAY FIRTH, Nairn is essentially a shore-fishing station. Most of the fishing is done from the two short piers at the entrance to the tidal harbour. Flatfish, cod, mackerel and the occasional pollack are the main species caught.

Lossiemouth

The visiting sea angler will probably find the Lossiemouth area fascinating, for to the south and east of the town most shore anglers concentrate on spinning for sea trout. These lovely sporting fish are caught right in the breakers on Toby lures and Mepps-type bar spoons. This is novelty fishing to most sea anglers and the Lossiemouth area is probably unique in this respect. Small-boat anglers in this area can catch sea trout, flatfish, haddock, cod, gurnard and small coalfish.

Buckie

Situated on the eastern side of SPEY BAY, Buckie has become a popular tourist resort in recent years. The entire shoreline to the east of the town is a good place to dig or gather bait. Worm or shellfish make the best baits in this area.

Portnockie, Portsoy, Banff and Rosehearty

These are all traditional fishing villages which still boast numerous commercial fishing boats. There is excellent rock, pier and beach fishing right along this extensive stretch of coastline. With ample facilities for launching small boats, this area has much to interest the boat angler, Mackerel, cod, haddock, flatfish, coalfish and the occasional skate make up the bulk of rod-caught catches in this area. Feathers are the favourite bait, although leger tackle should be used for the big plaice, dabs and skate.

Fraserburgh

Set on the north-east shoulder of Scotland, Fraserburgh has the Moray Firth to the north and the North Sea to the east. Basically a fishing port, Fraserburgh has also become something of a tourist resort in recent years. There are plenty of charter boats available in the harbour and small boats can also be launched.

Peterhead and Stonehaven

I have never found Peterhead or its adacent area to be particularly rich in fishing.

Stonehaven is a holiday resort situated fifteen miles south of Aberdeen in the centre of magnificent fishing country. Huge catches of cod and haddock are commonly taken in this area and the local club organises an annual sea-angling festival.

There is plenty of good rock fishing on either side of Stonehaven. Boat fishing off this section of coastline can produce some surprise catches in the shape of deep-sea catfish and hake. The catfish are ugly fish, armed with a mouthful of heavy teeth. Apart from these nasty-looking creatures and the beautiful though voracious hake, boats fishing out from Stonehaven bring in ling, skate, cod, haddock, conger eels, mackerel, flatfish and dogfish.

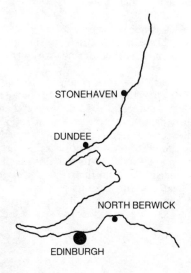

Dundee

Standing at the mouth of the River Tay, Dundee is surrounded on all sides by sea-fishing potential. Rock and pier fishing is possible at BROUGHTY FERRY, EAST HAVEN and

CARNOUSTIE. Shore fishing is best at RED HEAD, WHITINGNESS, CRAIL and ANSTRUTHER. Cod are the main fish caught by shore and pier anglers. Boat fishing around BELL ROCK and off NORTH CARR LIGHTHOUSE produces cod, haddock, small ling, pouting and flatfish.

Edinburgh to the Border

Edinburgh

The Firth of Forth is noted mainly for flatfish, codling and mackerel. The Edinburgh area is not rich in good fishing, although most local beaches can be relied upon to yield good supplies of worm and shellfish for bait.

North Berwick and Eyemouth

North Berwick is noted for the quality of its boat fishing. Cod, haddock, skate and flatfish are the most common species to be encountered, and thornback ray are particularly common.

Eyemouth, basically a rock-fishing centre, also provides fair boat-fishing opportunities. The rock fishing yields a wide variety of fish including cod, coalfish, mackerel and, in sandy areas, flatfish. I have had some good catches of coalfish in this area while using a German sprat-type artificial lure. This bait is heavy enough to cast a considerable distance which is a great advantage for I find that coalfish tend to concentrate 50 yards or so out from the rocks. A few years ago, a commercial boat trawling for prawns off ST ABB'S HEAD brought in a conger eel weighing 150 lb, nearly half as big again as the present specimen record for this species.

CHAPTER 11

North East Coast

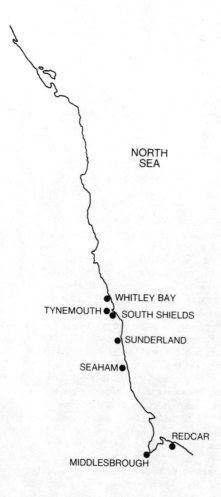

Tynemouth to Middlesbrough

This whole section of the north-east coast is capable of producing exceptional catches of shore-caught fish. As fishing grounds go, it is a rough, tough venue which calls for heavy tackle and a total disregard as far as lost terminal gear is concerned. Most local anglers cut costs by making their own weights and heavy nylon paternoster rigs. North-east-coast fishing is good, but like most places it takes time to learn local techniques and tricks. The angler willing to watch points and pick up snippets of information on terminal rigs and bait presentation will catch far more fish than the angler who works on the 'chuck-and-chance-it' principle.

Whitley Bay

Any angler who reads the news items or match results in the popular angling press will have heard of Whitley Bay and its potential. Whitley fishes best in the winter months when the winter codling move inshore to feed in the kelp-lined rock gullies that abound throughout the bay. Some anglers firmly believe that winter is the only time that Whitley Bay is worth fishing. This is far from true, for a few codling can always be found in the area around the kelp beds. Coalfish are present at all times of the year and localised sandy areas within the bay fish fairly well for plaice and dabs.

Mackerel, of course, can turn up during the summer months, although in recent seasons these visits have been rather spasmodic. Local specialists invariably fish the Whitley Bay marks on the first half of the ebb tide up to the first half of the flood tide. At these times conditions are right to drop a bait into the most productive gullies.

The varying nature of the shoreline means that even in bad weather there is always some section of shoreline that can be fished. All sections are likely to produce good codling. Although low water conditions are the most favoured, one or two places also fish well at high tide, so it is possible to fish somewhere within the area, irrespective of prevailing tidal conditions. Places to head for are ROCKY ISLAND at SEATON SLUICE where rock scarps or ledges provide good comfortable fishing stations. A high ledge known as the

SUMP is a good all-round mark. This ledge produces reasonable year-round fishing at all states of the tide and is therefore popular with visiting anglers and locals alike.

South of Seaton Sluice at COLLYWELL BAY vast beds of heavy kelp weed provide the visiting cod shoals with both a safe retreat and a well stocked larder. The cod caught here often run into double figures. Local anglers fishing this area usually head for MIDDLE SCAUR or ROUND ROCKS. At the southern extremity of Collywell Bay, CRAG POINT provides a good high-water cliff mark that fishes well in rough weather, but it is not a place for the nervous angler. On a north or north-easterly blow, HARTLEY SCAUR can produce good bags of codling on an ebb tide but basically fishing at this point is patchy.

ST MARY'S ISLAND is another kelp-filled area which is extremely popular with local anglers. Apart from the usual codling this rough, weed-covered mark occasionally produces wrasse and the odd pouting or two. St Mary's Island is connected to the mainland by a short causeway, access to the island being possible from approximately two hours either side of the top of the tide. Another cod hot-spot noted for the high proportion of double-figured fish it produces, is situated in a 200-yard stretch north of the boat station. Again this area fishes best when a north-easterly sea is running.

Whitley Bay Beach, roughly one and a half miles in length is a sandy beach interspersed with outcrops of rock. Casting out to these rock patches can be most productive with good-sized codling and coalfish providing most of the action. LITTLE BAY, a narrow gully at the extreme end of the North Promenade, is a good place to take flounders on an ebb tide. WATTS SLOPE, BIG BAY, NORTH WILKINSONS, THE PANAMA, and WHITLEY PIPE are all popular and well-known fishing spots. Any local angler will tell you the exact locality of these marks. Whitley Pipe is a comfortable flat rock stance which allow anglers to cast into fairly deep water. Most of the local specialists seem to congregate at the end of the Pipe but good catches can be taken at the bend. This particular mark can generally be relied on to fish well at any time of the year. Great caution should be used when fishing the end of the Pipe for fishing conditions become rather dangerous if any sort of sea is running.

Whitley Bay is something of a shore fisherman's paradise.

133

Practically any section of the bay can fish well and noted marks are numerous. The South Promenade and a rock mark known as the CHAIR are both good high-water venues which allow for comfortable fishing positions at all times. CRAWLEYS, a noted rock point situated beside the disused Table Rock Swimming Pool is very popular locally, yielding coalfish and fair codling. BROWN'S BAY and MARCONI POINT also fish well on high water, whereas NORTH CRAB HILL to the south of the Brown's Bay Lagoon is essentially a low-water station. Great care should be taken here for it is easy to become too engrossed in the fishing and not notice the incoming tide.

One of the main advantages of the Whitley Bay marks is that they can be fished comfortably by anglers with only average casting ability. This gives even the absolute shore-casting novice every opportunity of catching good fish. Heavy gear is essential. Local experts favour stiff-actioned 12-ft rods and massive, Scarborough-style centre-pin reels loaded with 35- or 40-lb b.s. line. Single-hook paternoster gear incorporating a length of weaker line between lead and paternoster swivel (see fig. 14) is the best rig to use. Even with this simple outfit, snags occur so you must be prepared to lose a fair amount of end tackle. Size 3–0 to 5–0 hooks are favoured for codling, but on flatfish marks smaller, long-shanked hooks should be employed.

For general fishing lug and ragworm make the best baits. During the winter months mussel is an effective cod bait and peeler or soft-backed crab, when obtainable, is the best bait of all. Lugworm can be dug at the north end of Whitley Bay Beach or obtained from local bait diggers or tackle dealers. Crabs and mussels have to be gathered from rocks. Small boats can be launched by the private boat compound. Cod, small whiting, coalfish, haddock and mackerel are the main quarry of the boat fishermen in this area. A leash of three baited feathers is the best terminal rig to use.

Tynemouth

South of Whitley Bay, Tynemouth produces good fishing to anglers who know where to fish. Cod, flounder, dab, plaice, pouting, whiting and dogfish can all be caught in the Tynemouth area. Like Whitley Bay, Tynemouth has many shore marks to choose from. The long sands to the south of CULLERCOATS, STONY BOTTOM, BARGE BOTTOM, KING EDWARD'S BAY, TYNEMOUTH HAVEN, SHARPNESS POINT and CULLERCOATS HARBOUR are all good shore fishing points giving access to a wide variety of fish.

For anglers who enjoy pier fishing, the estuary, fish quay wall and HOWDEN STAITHES make good casting platforms. Boat fishing in the area is reasonably good, particularly for cod and coalfish. Ragworm, lugworm and the locally-favoured white worm can be dug in the Tyne estuary. Bait digging here is hard work.

South Shields

Directly across from Tynemouth, South Shields offers similar opportunities for sport. Local anglers are inclined to fish the one-and-a-half-mile-long pier regularly and when fish are on the move, this pier can produce excellent catches. Shore fishing marks like SOUTH BEACH, HERD BEACH, BLACK ROCK, WHITE ROCK, BLOW HOLE and CAMMIS ISLAND WALL are also worth trying. FRENCHMAN'S POINT, although a fairly good spot, can be a very dangerous place to fish, so my advice is to leave this mark well alone unless you have a full understanding of tides.

Sunderland

Very little boat fishing is done in the Sunderland area although the offshore marks can fish fairly well. Private boats operating from NORTH DOCKS sometimes bring in good catches of codling and dogfish from offshore marks but little has been done to develop the boat-fishing potential of the area.

Shore fishing is fairly good. RYHOPE BEACH, the estuary of the RIVER WEAR, LIZARD POINT, all fish well enough at times. Bass occasionally occur in this area, although most catches are made up of codling and small flatfish. SEABURN PROMENADE and ROKER PIER are good places to head for during the winter months, with codling being the main catch.

Seaham

The farther south one comes, the more varied the fish become. At Seaham, for example, boat anglers get skate and conger as well as codling, dogfish, mackerel, pouting and the usual flatfish. No one specifically organises boat fishing at Seaham but local boat owners will take out occasional parties on request.

Shore fishing is the most popular form of angling here and marks such as HAIL BEACH to the north of Seaham and BLAST BEACH to the south are favoured venues. The NORTH PIER is also very popular, particularly during the winter months, when shoals of codling and whiting put in a regular appearance. Like most places in the north-east, charter-boat trips are difficult to arrange, although anglers launching their own boats can find good sport all along this section of coastline. Catches of twenty or more good-sized codling are commonly made by inshore-boat fishermen. Baited feathers on a two-hook paternoster rig baited with mussels, worms or fish cuttings should be used.

Redcar

Shore fishing in the Redcar area is good but often dangerous. The COATHAM and REDCAR ROCKS are favourite venues but the surrounding shallow water troughs tend to fill rapidly on an incoming tide and unless great care is taken it is easy to become cut off from safety in a remarkably short space of time. A sandy patch near the Coatham Hotel provides a safe beach fishing stance, although fishing at this point is rather patchy. The SOUTH GARE BREAKWATER and SALTBURN PIER are worth trying. Charter boats are virtually non-existent in Redcar and Middlesbrough, but inshore fishing is good.

CHAPTER 12

The Yorkshire Coast

The rugged coastline of Yorkshire, with its vast cliffs, jutting rock ledges and weed-encrusted rocks, can usually be relied upon to produce some good sport for the keen sea angler. Shore fishing here is a long-established recreation and over the years local anglers have developed a highly characteristic style of angling that consistently catches fish from areas which would appear at first sight to be totally unfishable. The coastline is a challenge to the skill and endurance of any angler. The fish are there in plenty. All it takes to catch them is know-how, perseverance and a total disregard for weather and sea conditions.

In terms of geographical layout and fish population, the Yorkshire coastline is divided into two sections. North of FLAMBOROUGH HEAD is rough, tough rock fishing where cod are the main fish caught. South of Bridlington the shoreline changes considerably. Rocks give way to sandy, easy-accessible beaches. Cod are still caught in this area but they are not so common. Instead thornback ray, dabs and even tope can be taken. This softer section of coastline can produce good shore fishing but it is better known as a boat-fishing area.

Whitby

In the north of the county, this resort caters for sea angling in a big way. Boats are readily available in the Whitby

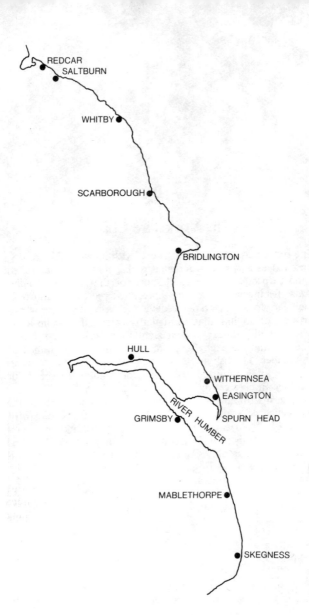

area, mostly for cod fishing. Cod are the mainstay of sport all along the Yorkshire coastline and it is interesting to note that boat catches do not always exceed shore catches, particularly in terms of quality of fish caught rather than sheer quantity. Despite the fact that cod are the most commonly-caught species on the Yorkshire coast, the average size of fish is well below the average for cod caught in southern waters. A 20-lb Yorkshire-caught cod is a veritable monster by local standards, whereas a fish of this size caught off the Kent coast, for example, would be regarded as a reasonable but by no means exceptional specimen. Codling (small cod in the 3-lb to 7-lb range), are extremely prolific and boat anglers fishing known Yorkshire cod grounds can reasonably expect to catch fish of this size by the boxfull. Cod over 10 lb are, however, a much scarcer breed and it is here that the shore, or rather rock, fisherman often scores. The larger cod seem to come close inshore to take full advantage of the rich feeding-grounds round the rock ledges on which anglers normally stand. A favourite spot in the Whitby area is SALTWICK NAB just south of the town.

Ravenscar and Scarborough

This is another area well worth visiting. Good boat fishing can be found all along this section of coastline and boat trips can be arranged from all the main resorts. The Scarborough area is extremely rich for the shore angler: SCALBY NESS, JACKSON'S BAY and CLOUGHTON are firm favourites with local anglers and visitors alike and on the days when the cod shoals are in and weather conditions are suitable, some great catches can be made. Yorkshire anglers are as hardy a breed as you will find anywhere in the British Isles. Any section of coastline which has any form of access, no matter how dangerous the descent may be, will be hard-fished solidly throughout the entire year. Local anglers also occasionally fish directly from the tops of the towering cliffs. This is not to be recommended, particularly where visiting anglers are concerned, for unless you know the terrain extremely well, this spectacular cliff-hanging style of angling can be extremely dangerous.

Filey Brigg

A huge natural breakwater on the extremity of Filey Bay, this is a vast natural pier giving rock fishermen every opportunity to scramble out along its rugged length to cast into particularly productive waters.

Bridlington

Fishing trips on local boats are easy to arrange from here and extremely popular, for catches are often exceptionally good, although big fish are far from common. This whole coastline is capable of producing surprise catches. Beach anglers find the occasional medium-sized bass, boat anglers may encounter that ugly cold-water monster, the catfish, with its slippery body, ungainly head and lethal-looking jaws. Porbeagle shark are known to visit this coastline and of course it must be remembered that at one time Scarborough held the world record for the blue-fin tunny. Huge tunny were once common off the Yorkshire coast and big-game fishermen from all over the world made a habit of visiting Scarborough to take full advantage of the migrating tunny packs. Of course, tunny can still be caught off Yorkshire, but the high cost of hiring suitable boats and the near extinction of the once-prolific herring shoals on which the tunny fed means that tunny fishing as a sport is too chancy and too expensive for the average angler to indulge in.

During the period between the wars, tunny fishing here reached its peak, catches were high and fish of between 500 and 700 lb were commonplace. An attempt was made after the Second World War to re-establish tunny fishing as a sport, but by this time commercial harvesting of the herring shoals had taken its toll of the tunny's main food supply. A few fish were caught, but nothing was seen of the vast packs of big tunny that once frequented the area, and local sportsmen reluctantly gave up the idea of tunny hunting as a productive pastime. Tunny apart, the Yorkshire coastline holds some wonderful fishing, with a wide choice of venues to try and fish to catch.

Yorkshire Tackle

There is nothing fine about the average Yorkshire angler's tackle. Long and costly experience, fishing over really rough, line-chaffing rock into beds of rope-stemmed kelp weed has taught the Yorkshire man to use tackle that would under normal circumstances stop a runaway elephant.

For years, favourite rock-fishing gear consisted of a great thick Burma pole rod, a huge wooden Scarborough-type centre-pin reel and 60- to 80-lb b.s. line. Modern anglers have now discarded much of this ultra-heavy gear in favour of glass-fibre beach-casting rods and multiplier reels. Despite this shift towards modern gear, the new tackle is still very heavy in comparison to south country gear. Beach-casters capable of throwing 8 to 10 oz of lead and 40- to 50-lb b.s. nylon can hardly be classed as normal shore-fishing tackle. Prevailing conditions on the rock-fishing stations of North Yorkshire dictate what sort of gear can be used if you hope to land the fish you hook. Make no mistake about it, an 8- or 10-lb cod hooked in a kelp-forest 60 to 80 yards out over razor-edged rocks takes some landing. Under these circumstances 40-lb lines can part like cotton and to land the fish you hook successfully, it is essential to use a set of gear which can lift, bully and finally winch every hooked fish over all the tackle-smashing obstructions which exist between the fishing grounds and the shore.

In the south of the county, where the rocks give way to sand, more conventional beach-casting tackle can be used without fear. As far as boat fishing is concerned, any standard boat outfit can be used, for big fish are the exception rather than the rule. Despite the fact that codling and small coalfish can often be hooked in at the rate of two or three at a time, a normal boat rod matched with 30-lb b.s. line will be quite strong enough to cope with the kind of fish and fishing that can be expected.

Specialised tackle

Yorkshire anglers are famous for having devised a practical set of terminal tackle known as *rotten-bottom gear*. This rotten-bottom tackle is made up on the paternoster principle with the lead being attached either by old,

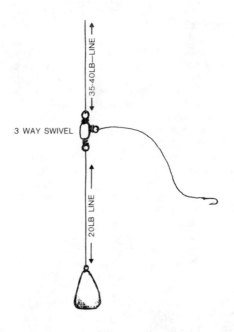

3 WAY SWIVEL

20LB LINE

Fig. 14   Rotten-bottom tackle.

rotten line or nowadays line of much lighter breaking
strain than the actual reel line. This peculiar type of gear
was developed specifically to cut down tackle losses while
fishing amongst thick weed and jagged rock, the idea being
that should the lead become wedged in a crevice or wrapped
round a strong stalk of kelp weed a good, hefty pull on the
rod would cause the weak or lighter line between lead and
terminal tackle to part, thus allowing the angler to retrieve
the bulk of his end tackle. If the lead was attached by line
of similar breaking strain to the reel line the chances are the
breakage would occur above rather than below the paternoster booms which would automatically double the cost
of the lost gear, waste valuable time and possibly even result
in the loss of a good fish. This last occurrence would not
happen with rotten-bottom gear, for should the weight become jammed while a fish is being played out, the light line

can be quickly broken, leaving the angler totally in control of the hooked fish.

Fishing a rocky coastline is invariably an expensive pastime and the rotten-bottom terminal rig of Yorkshire can be used anywhere where rocks and weed abound. I have used this style of end tackle in Cornwall, Scotland and Ireland and although lead losses have always been high, I have managed to save considerably by generally rescuing the business end of my terminal tackle.

The paternoster is the only really practical type of gear to use on the North Yorkshire coast. It keeps the bait up off the bottom, where feeding fish can see it and cuts down the

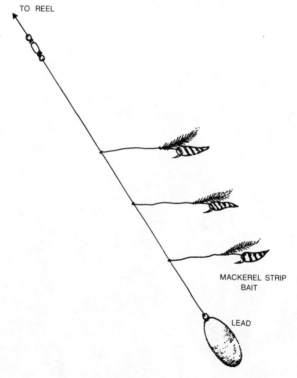

TO REEL

MACKEREL STRIP
BAIT

LEAD

Fig. 15. Baited cod feathers.

chances of snagging to an acceptable level. Certainly leger gear used in the same conditions would result in the tackle instantly fouling up on the bottom. On a flat, sandy bottom there is no point in using tackle of this sort and a leger or standard paternoster can be used. For boat fishing off the Yorkshire coast a string of three baited cod feathers (see fig. 15) is the favourite rig to use. The feathers with additional bait in the shape of fish-cuttings or worms make a deadly combination for most of the common local species.

CHAPTER 13

The East Coast

From the sandy beaches of Skegness down to the mud flats of the Thames estuary, the east coast can provide good fishing for a wide variety of species.

Many anglers who have never fished this section of coastline tend to regard it as a rather drab uninteresting area which does not hold much of interest for the big-fish hunter or the specialist angler. This is far from the truth. Like most stretches of coastline, the east coast from Skegness down to Southend can provide an interesting and very varied selection of species.

For the angler who just likes to go fishing for the pot, most of the venues are capable of producing medium-weight fish such as flounder, whiting, small skate and codling with the occasional sole catch thrown in to add interest and excitement to the fishing. Most east coast anglers have big fish stories to tell and although many of these big fish are lost through too light tackle or total inexperience, there are occasions when someone out after small fish does successfully catch a huge tope, bass or monster sting-ray. Big-fish hunters are, of course, constantly out after fish of this calibre and from ports like Hunstanton huge catches of fine tope are often made. Hunstanton holds a regular Tope Festival where anglers from all over the country and the continent meet and compete for the various prizes and trophies involved. Individual catches of up to eight or ten tope per man have been made during these contests and the whole of the Wash area holds plenty of potential for any boat angler who wishes to try his luck with this exciting, hard-fighting little shark.

Big cod are fairly common throughout the entire length of this coastline. Farther south the mud flats of Essex hold monster sting-ray and a plentiful supply of heavyweight smooth hound. Both fish normally fall to worm baits, although on occasions the larger sting-ray pick up fish baits intended originally for tope. Worm baits also produce some excellent Essex bass catches and most anglers in this area are practising conservationists who return the bulk of their bass catches alive to the water.

Quite apart from these fish, the area can occasionally produce some reasonable conger eels. Normally conger are regarded as accidental catches and I have never yet met an east coast angler who goes out fishing specifically for them.

Skegness to Southend

Skegness

The sea wall and pier can produce plenty of action, particularly during the high water period when fish come inshore to feed on worms and other food. Some local anglers use strips of fresh herring as a substitute for worm, although generally speaking lugworms dug locally produce the bulk of the good catches for beach and pier anglers. Sandbanks and extremely shallow water make boat angling in the Skegness area rather difficult. Farther south, at King's Lynn, fishing is rather prohibited and apart from river fishing for silver eels and flounders, shore anglers have little opportunity of finding good sport.

King's Lynn

The boat angler however, can get out from King's Lynn to fish the famed Wash tope and thornback skate marks. Tope fishing in this area can be extremely good and large catches of these fine fighting fish can be taken during the summer months.

Hunstanton

With its sandy beaches and fine pier, HUNSTANTON can produce some remarkably good catches of flatfish, whiting, silver eels and the occasional cod or codling. Lugworm can be dug locally and the area fishes well in all but a strong north-west wind which when coupled with the prevailing tide flows, makes fishing impossible. HEACHAM and HOLKHAM beaches are favourite venues with local and visiting anglers.

Sheringham

The rocky shoreline and pier produce good catches of flatfish, whiting and cod. Boat fishing in this area can produce plenty of big bags, although individual fish seldom achieve specimen weights. The noted shore marks of the area are WEYBOURNE, CLEY and SALTHOUSE BEACHES.

147

Wells

The large fishing fleet based here provides ample opportunity for boat fishing and the many channels and holes in the sea bottom can provide excellent tope and skate fishing.

Cromer

Like most coastlines the east coast changes considerably throughout its length, one area provides good flatfishing, another offers the opportunity of bigger fish. Cromer combines both. Best known for its pier and beach fishing, Cromer is famous for sole and, oddly enough, big tope. More than one 40-lb-plus tope has been caught by a beach or pier angler fishing with big baits, and it would seem likely that these big fish come inshore to take advantage of the flatfish shoals that browse over the area. A favourite spot here is the east end of the beach where sandy spots surrounded by rock provide flatfish with food and shelter from marauding predators.

From Cromer round to Great Yarmouth the beaches at WALCOTT, BACTON, MUNDESLEY, HORSEY, HEMSBY, WINTERTON and CAISTER are all good places to fish. Unfortunately during the holiday season the over-spill from nearby holiday camps can make these beaches too crowded to fish, although night-fishing sessions to any of these beaches can ge productive. I like to visit this area during the winter-time when small codling are plentiful and each cast brings the chance of making contact with a 20-lb-plus cod. During various parts of the year whiting, dabs, sole, flounders and good skate can be caught from these beaches. I remember a night-fishing session on this stretch of coastline when the thornback skate went on a mad feeding spree. Time after time, I cast big bunches of lugworm out and within minutes I felt the familiar hard knocking bite of a hungry thornback skate. I did not catch any really big thornbacks on this occasion but I did manage a dozen or so nice fish ranging from 6 lb to 9 lb in size. I also had the odd flatfish and a couple of truly diminutive little thornbacks which I carefully returned alive after unhooking. It is not often that a beach angler gets the chance of making a skate catch as large as this, although skate can be very numerous in this area at certain times of the year.

Great Yarmouth and Gorleston

These towns are usually packed with holiday-makers from June to late September. Even so, with nearly seven miles of beach, roughly two miles of quays and three piers, the shore angler has plenty of opportunity to practice his sport. Boat fishing from the harbour or from the beach provides excellent opportunities to avoid holiday crowds and with good fishing at almost any time of the year, the whole area makes an ideal angling base.

Lowestoft

Another excellent centre with good sandy beaches, and two piers providing plenty of scope for local and visiting anglers alike. In the yacht basin close to the harbour entrance it is possible to catch flounders, silver eels, smelt and even good mullet although these latter fish are difficult to catch. Lowestoft, like Yarmouth is noted mainly for its autumn and winter cod fishing. During the autumn and early winter months, huge shoals of prime whiting also visit the area providing good catches for both boat and shore fishermen.

South of Lowestoft at PAKEFIELD and KESSINGLAND there is deep water close to the shore.

Southwold

Southwold boasts a good sandy beach, a short pier and a harbour. Being situated in a bay, the beach is practically tide-free, although at the harbour entrance the tide run is often so strong that it makes fishing well-nigh impossible. Anglers fishing here at slack water are often rewarded with good catches of fine sole. There are also bass in the bay although as a general rule they are far from plentiful. The whole area is capable of yielding bass of exceptional size, but most of these fish are caught accidentally on big baits intended for skate or tope. Occasionally someone fishing with light tackle for flatfish makes contact with a big bass. More often than not this results in a tackle breakage and the loss of the fish.

Aldeburgh

Farther along, the coast is a rather stony beach until it reaches the estuary of the Alde River. Often overcrowded with holiday-makers, this area fishes well throughout the year. Several small, isolated beaches north of the town fish well during the winter months, particularly for whiting and the occasional big cod.

Orford

Situated on the Alde estuary this is a good summer venue for skate fishing but to get to the best grounds it is necessary to cross the river. This can be arranged through the offices of the Harbour Master.

Felixtowe, Walton-on-the-Naze and Clacton-on-Sea

These are difficult places to fish during the summer months due to a massive influx of visitors. All three towns have good piers and beaches which vary from sand to large stones and mud patches. For boat fishing during the summer months, bass and thornback skate are the main species, while in the winter months cod and whiting can be caught from beaches and boats alike. Felixstowe produced the original bass record.

Harwich to Frinton-on-Sea

Basically good fishing centres, these venues fish well at times for most of the common east coast species.

Blackwater and Crouch

The coast off these rivers dries out with extensive mud and sandbanks, and is best explored in many boat trips with an experienced fisherman. Alternatively charter trips are available. The estuaries themselves provide some excellent fishing, including bass at the right time of the tide. *Estuary Fishing,* by Frank Holiday, in the ANGLER'S LIBRARY, is recommended reading for suitable methods.

Southend, Canvey Island and the Thames Estuary

This whole area can provide good summer and winter fishing and a wide variety of fish. Quite apart from the normal flounders, silver eels, cod, bass and skate, this section of the Essex coastline has in recent seasons produced a steady stream of more unusual fish. Heavyweight sting-ray can often be encountered and beach and inshore-boat anglers often make contact with good, big smooth hounds. The Thames estuary up as far as GRAVESEND is now, thanks to a gradual cleaning-up process of the river, producing excellent results. Winter cod and flounder fishing is particularly good and a year or two ago the whole area began to produce excellent haddock catches. These have now diminished again but local anglers feel that the haddock shoals could re-appear at any time to add interest and weight to boat angler's catches. The whole of the Thames estuary is wide open for exploration. As yet only a fraction of its potential has been discovered and there is a great deal of scope for any angler, particularly those who can get afloat, to discover and develop the potential of this fascinating area to the full.

Equipment for East Coast Fishing

Bait

Lugworm is by far the most popular of all east coast baits. On many sections of this coastline it is the only bait that can be relied upon to catch fish consistently. Lugworm can be dug or bought at many places along the east coast, consequently there is rarely a bait shortage. East coast anglers use lugworms either singly or in bunches of anything up to half a dozen. Single worms on small size 1 or 1–0 long-shanked hooks are good baits for flatfish and whiting, while bunches of worms can be used to take skate, cod, sting-ray, bass and big smooth hounds. East coast skate and cod are particularly fond of a good meal of lugworms and most of the big catches taken on the east coast fall to this bait.

Obviously, worms do not interest tope very much and most tope fishermen stick exclusively to fish baits of one sort or another. Fillets of herring or mackerel are the most popular baits, although small flatfish used whole have accounted for many large Wash-caught tope. Small strips of herring and mackerel can also be used to take cod and whiting, but this bait is inferior to lugworm for these species.

For the boat angler who does not mind spending time collecting bait, a fish-baited drop net can be used to secure a good supply of hermit crabs. Once removed from their adopted shells, these hard-headed, soft-bodied little crabs make a good all-round bait. Smooth hound are particularly fond of these juicy little crustaceans and many of the more successful Essex smooth-hound specialists use this bait to the exclusion of all other locally available baits.

For the energetic bait collectors, soft-back or peeler crab can be found in some areas. These are particularly good fish catchers and are well worth the trouble of gathering.

Tackle

With one or two exceptions east coast marks are remarkably snag-free. For this reason, and the fact that most species other than tope are caught mainly on small baits, east coast anglers tend to fish rather light. For beach, pier and general shore fishing lines of 20 lb b.s. are quite sufficient and for boat work it is unnecessary to fish with line of more than 30 lb b.s.

Beach fishermen in this area prefer long castings, as the shallow water keeps the fish well offshore. Beach-casting rods of 12 ft or more are standard equipment. Rods capable of casting 4 oz to 8 oz of lead should be used.

Boat anglers require nothing special in the way of rods, needing only the standard 6-ft models for the larger species.

For tope, skate, sting-ray and smooth hound, leger tackle should be used. Whiting and cod fall to bait presented on a nylon paternoster terminal gear.

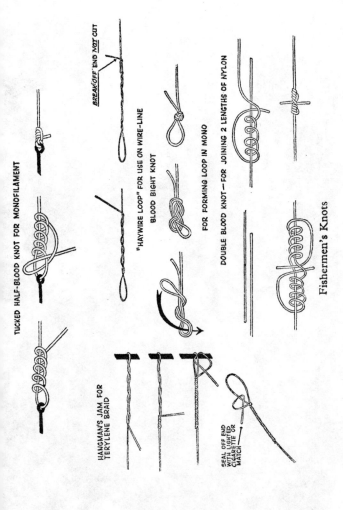

TUCKED HALF-BLOOD KNOT FOR MONOFILAMENT

BREAK-OFF END *NOT* CUT

"HAYWIRE LOOP" FOR USE ON WIRE-LINE

BLOOD BIGHT KNOT

FOR FORMING LOOP IN MONO

DOUBLE BLOOD KNOT—FOR JOINING 2 LENGTHS OF NYLON

HANGMAN'S JAM FOR TERYLENE BRAID

SEAL OFF END WITH LIGHTED CIGARETTE OR MATCH

Fishermen's Knots

Selective Index

Most fish appear throughout the text. References are only given for pages on which they receive special mention for size, good fishing, etc.